BEYOND 2012:

WHAT THE REAL PROPHETS ARE SAYING

by Julia Loren

BEYOND 2012: WHAT THE REAL PROPHETS ARE SAYING...

Tharseo Publishing (thar-Say-o)
370 NE Camano Dr.
Suite 5, PMB 4
Camano Island, WA 98282
www.divineinterventionbooks.com

I Hear the Prophets Saying...

Book Disclaimer

The opinions expressed by the contributors and those quoted are theirs alone, and do not reflect the opinions of the other contributors, or of various readers. The contributing authors are not necessarily endorsing either the views, or the ministries, of all other contributors.

The information provided in this book is designed to provide helpful information on the subjects discussed. This book is not meant to be used, nor should it be used, to influence your life decisions. Predictive and futuristic words and views should never be utilized in real-world decisions. Take them to prayer and listen on your own.

This book is designed to provide information and motivation to our readers. It is sold with the understanding that the publisher is not engaged to render any type of psychological, legal, or any other kind of professional advice. The content of each article is the sole expression and opinion of its author, and not necessarily that of the publisher or of the other contributors. No warranties or guarantees are expressed or implied by the publisher's choice to include any of the content in this volume. Neither the publisher nor the individual author(s)/contributors shall be liable for any physical, psychological, emotional, financial, or commercial damages, including, but not limited to, special, incidental, consequential or other damages. Our views and rights are the same: You are responsible for your own choices, actions, and results.

The Lord's Prayer

(Translated from the Aramaic by Dr. Neil Douglas-Klotz)

O, Birther of the Cosmos, focus your light within us
— make it useful.
Create your reign of unity now.
Your one desire then acts with ours,
As in all light,
So in all forms,
Grant us what we need each day in bread and insight:
Loose the cords of mistakes binding us,
As we release the strands we hold of others' guilt.
Don't let surface things delude us,
But free us from what holds us back.
From you is born all ruling will,
The power and the life to do,
The song that beautifies all,
From age to age it renews.
I affirm this with my whole being.

TABLE OF CONTENTS

TABLE OF CONTENTS CONT....

INTRODUCTION

Since the early days of creation the earth has experienced upheavals and natural disasters. These natural disasters split landmasses into continents, formed islands in the sea, and developed the planet into something humans could inhabit, subdue, and steward. It is a living planet. Natural disasters still occur. Whole regions shift and quake.

Throughout history, God gifted men and women with the ability to draw so close to Him that they became friends, living in an ongoing conversation with the Creator who told them about events to come. Those who were close to God were called "prophets". Their purpose was to encourage and speak to the Church, to prepare them for the days to come, to draw the hearts of the people to know a loving God, their Creator. Those who sought revelation outside of the boundaries of their relationship with God and Jesus Christ were called "diviners", "mediums", and "spiritists" who operated not through the spirit of God, the Holy Spirit. Their purpose was to lead the culture at large astray and into the darkness of fear and depression. That mixture still exists in our culture; a mixture that includes shifting shadows of light and darkness. As the darkness grows darker, the light shines ever brighter. Yet a battle is taking place—spiritually as well as naturally, for the nations of earth and the lands and seas reflect what occurs in the heavens.

This book contains the voices of the friends of God known to our American culture for their depth of relationship with God, the accuracy of the words God speaks to them and through them, and the integrity of their ministries. They are respected Christian prophets in our culture, most of them well known for decades. The foundation of their theology is the cross of Christ and their perspectives diverge and converge from one another—even as ours do.

My intent in compiling their words and releasing them to the Church in this book, is to prepare the body of Christ to connect with the head—Jesus—so that we may live in tune with His thoughts and His peace, deeply encompassed in His love during the days to come. I want to combat the climate of fear that has stretched over the earth due to economic woes and natural disasters and "end-times" theology that believes that God is getting ready to demolish the earth and punish people, judging them for their sins. We can be prepared for the difficulties of life and live with our hearts at peace and even rise up to a higher level of authority that will calm not only the inner storms but outer storms with the power of Christ in us. These prophetic voices will lead you there.

We are living in a season of grace still. I trust that as you read, that grace will wash over you, reignite your love and desire to know Jesus better, and calm your fears. In this world we have always had trouble. But take heart, Christ has overcome the world and is preparing us to rise above it all—with Him.

- Julia C. Loren

http://iheartheprophets.wordpress.com/

SORTING

THROUGH

REVELATION

REAL PROPHECY BUILDS FAITH, NOT FEAR

by Marc Dupont

The gift of prophecy holds a unique place amongst the list of spiritual gifts Paul discussed in his first letter to the church of Corinth. Unique due to two reasons: One, it is the most to be sought after, according to Paul; and two, it is by far the most controversial gifts in the eyes of the contemporary church. Controversial to the point that even many church leaders who believe in prophecy today refuse to allow prophecy, or even prophetic training, within their congregations.

Being a teacher of intimacy with God for almost three decades I am more than enthusiastic regarding the gift of prophecy. However, I somewhat understand the position of those leaders who value the gift but allow no place for the gift to develop in their churches. I understand their dilemma because many so-called 'prophetic ministries' are caught up in two very serious pitfalls. One, some fail to use the Bible to set a standard for prophecy. Subsequently their prophetic words sometimes do not reflect Biblical values. Secondly, too many prophetic ministries have either superficial or a complete lack of accountability with their lives and the words they give out.

I wrote the following article over ten years ago due to the first problem with current prophetic voices. The problem surfaced in a huge way back in 1998-1999. As many computer experts began to predict severe economic problems due to massive worldwide computer failure worldwide with the turning of the computer clocks from 1999 to 2000, many prophetic voices jumped on the "doom & gloom" bandwagon.

Many people—Christian and non—bought generators, stored up water and food, and prepared for the worst-case scenario. Obviously, the dire predictions/prophecies never panned out. The following article was written in response:

Real Prophecy brings Faith, Not Fear

Of all the spiritual gifts Paul wrote about in his letter to the Church of Corinth in 1 Corinthians 12-14, he highlighted prophecy as the gift that a believer should first seek. I believe he did this for a reason. The other gifts, with the exception of some use of tongues, are primarily for the work of the Kingdom, tools for ministry. Prophecy, however, enables us to hear what God desires to speak to the Church. In fact, Paul prayed for the Church of Ephesus to have "*the Spirit of wisdom and revelation, so that you may know Him* (the Father) *better*" (Ephesians 1:17 NIV).

Prophecy leads to greater intimacy with God. It can take us out of the religious posture of attempting to do what we think God would have us do by helping us to understand the Father's specific will and direction. When we study the life of Jesus, we see that He only did the things He saw the Father doing. (See John 5:19-20, 8:28-29.) It means the difference between "good ideas" and "God ideas." To quote Thomas Hohstadt, it is the difference between "lightening and the lightening bug."

Prophecy also helps us to see things from God's perspective rather than from our human understanding. For example, it is easy to focus on the amount of sin and destruction, idolatry, and violence in the world today and have a dim hope for the increase of the gospel. But when we lift up the eyes of our hearts to God, we see that nothing shall be impossible for God and that He truly is "Lord of the harvest."

One problem, however, is that sometimes the prophet's limited wholeness and/or Bible knowledge filters the revelation he receives and strongly influences his interpretation of what he experiences. When our hearts are right with God and resting in Him, we see and hear what the Holy Spirit shows us. This builds faith and confidence in what God wants to do. But when we have fear and uneasiness or a weak theology concerning such things as the sovereignty of God, we cloud the revelation with our own weaknesses.

During the 70s and 80s, several Norwegian pastors and church leaders began to see similar visions and dreams of what appeared to be blood flowing down a map of Norway. It started from northern Norway where it bordered the former Soviet Union and then flowed to southern Norway. At that time the Soviets housed a large army and several naval bases around Murmansk near the northern border of Norway. The Norwegians were afraid of the Soviet "superpower" that had already taken over many nearby nations in Eastern Europe. Because of their fear of one day being invaded from the north by the Soviets, many Norwegians interpreted the vision negatively. Unless the church of Norway prayed with great diligence, the country was going to be overrun by the Soviets as their Eastern bloc neighbors had been in years past. The bloodstained map represented to them the lives of the Norwegians that would be lost in this invasion.

Those praying Christians are to be commended for their faith, but what really happened, however, was quite different. About the time of "glasnost" and "peristroika" during the late 80s, a strong move of the Holy Spirit began in the northern Soviet Union after nearly 70 years of enforced atheism. Instead of being destroyed many Norwegian churches and leaders became deeply involved in a wonderful move of the Holy Spirit in the country they had always feared. Several large cities and different ethnic groups who had not heard the gospel for generations began to respond to Jesus.

As the move of the Holy Spirit grew, many churches in Norway who were involved in this fresh move of the Spirit began to experience a fresh dynamic move of the Holy Spirit, also. They began to reap what they were sowing in another place. Finally they realized that what God had been saying to them was not what they had feared, but rather the "blood of the Lamb" was beginning to flow along the northern border and then south through the entire nation of Norway!

TESTING WORDS OF PROPHECY

Due to our tendency to filter words from God through human perspective it is critical that we apply several tests to them. First of all, is the word, dream, or vision consistent with scriptural themes? It's not enough that a "word" contain a Bible verse, or spiritual symbols. It must be consistent with the doctrine and spirit of the Bible. For example, a word that manipulates the hearers to give offerings out of obligation would be inconsistent with Paul's directive to give out of a joyful heart. (See 2 Corinthians 9:7)

Next, does the word come to pass? The Holy Spirit speaks perfectly while we hear imperfectly. While recognizing that no one except the Lord is infallible, we must still apply Biblical standards. This is why Paul exhorted us to "weigh" or judge prophecies. Someone with a recognized prophetic ministry should consistently prophesy with accuracy rather than continually giving what amounts to "false prophecies" that never comes to pass. I believe that there is another sort of false prophecy that is very evident within the church today. It comes from those who accurately prophesy things to come but give a false reflection of God the Father. There are, unfortunately, prophets who sensationalize words of judgment, destruction, and gloom but without giving any hope and encouragement to the church. The short-term fruit of these so-called "words" is fear and a lack of faith. The long-term effects of these "words" are apathy toward real words from God and potentially a lack of Holy Spirit inspired vision for the future.

Certainly God does, at times, give words of warning and subsequent directions for prayer. True prophecy, however, always produces peace, hope, and comfort in knowing that God is good and in control! Paul wrote that God's intention in giving us prophetic words, visions, and dreams was to encourage, strengthen, and comfort us (1 Corinthians 14:3) and to help us see things from God's perspective. And according to the Bible, God is always working things out for the good of those who love Him (Romans 8:28). In fact, even during times of famine the Bible promises that the righteous will have abundance for every good work (Psalm 37:19). God the Father allows nothing to take place in our lives that is not shaped by His kindness for us. This, by no means, negates the fact that God does allow those whom He loves to suffer. It does mean, however, that prophecy, when revealing difficulties, should point to God's redemptive and kind purposes for each of us.

During the last several years I have heard many prophecies released to the church that have caused more harm than good. Many of these words prophesied great collapses of society and economic turmoil taking place at the turn of the millennium because of Y2K computer problems. Others have prophesied that parts of the U.S. would experience devastating earthquakes that would practically decimate entire cities and even states. There have been several words about other major nationwide disasters such as nuclear bombings in the U.S.

Many of these words have been characterized by sensationalism, which both the secular and Christian culture seem to constantly demand, and a lack of God's redemptive purposes. Not only were most of these words unfulfilled but they have produced bad fruit in some churches. Could it be that just as the secular news industry understands that bad news sells, the Christian "prophetic news industry" is also trying to sell a product?

EXAMINING THE FRUIT

Widespread acceptance of these "words" produced bad fruit in three ways. First, some Christians took their eyes off the Lord of the harvest and allowed themselves to be "derailed" from a focus on the Kingdom of God as being an ever-increasing Kingdom. Second, many Christians have somehow forgotten the wonderful promises of Jesus to be with us and for us. Third, "words" like these have caused many people to completely distrust all prophetic words, even those that are genuine which God gives to bring vision, hope, and direction.

In many places of the world such as parts of Asia, Africa, and South America, cities and nations are experiencing a great harvest. I also believe that God has been preparing churches in North America and Europe for the last 25 years for such moves of the Holy Spirit. As part of that process, God has restored prophetic ministry to the Church to strengthen her.

Some would say that these "judgment" prophecies were true words from God but because the church has prayed, God has withheld his hand of judgment. Although this may be true in some cases, we need to realize that in the last few years there has been an unprecedented amount of prayer made on behalf of our nations. Thousands of churches and leaders are taking to heart Solomon's encouraging words for any nation facing great difficulty because of its sin.

If my people, who are called by my name, will humble themselves and pray and seek my face and turn from their wicked ways, then will I hear from heaven and will forgive their sin and will heal their land. (2 Chronicles 7:14)

According to His word, in the face of brokenness and humility, God will answer prayers and continue to pour out His Spirit. It's a time for us to seek His glory, not His wrath!

As we continue to seek God for our nations, let us continue to lift up the eyes of our hearts to see that the harvest fields are ripe. Let's continue to seek after the Lord of the harvest for laborers for the harvest and trust Him that because He is a good Father, He speaks to His children to bring encouragement, strength, and comfort rather than fear of the future. Let's remember Isaiah's prophecy:

> I, the LORD, have called you in righteousness; I will take hold of your hand. I will keep you and will make you to be a covenant for the people and a light for the Gentiles, to open eyes that are blind, to free captives from prison and to release from the dungeon those who sit in darkness. I am the LORD; that is my name! I will not give my glory to another or my praise to idols. See, the former things have taken place, and new things I declare; before they spring into being I announce them to you. (Isaiah 42:6-9)

3 DANGEROUS PHENOMENA IN CURRENT PROPHETIC MINISTRY

I have had the opportunity of being involved with prophetic and apostolic ministries internationally for close to 3 decades. I count myself the richer and wiser for this privilege of rubbing shoulders with many men and women who God has spoken through to the body of Christ in wonderful ways with wonderful messages of encouragement and exhortation.

Unfortunately, over the last decade, or so, I have also seen the current prophetic movement both become more extreme and more irrelevant to true Biblical Kingdom purposes. I believe there are three specific harmful phenomena that have emerged which are much in evidence today. They are:

- A Phenomenal focus on self-promotion
- A Phenomenal lack of self-accountability

- A Phenomenal emphasis on phenomena, to the cost of de-emphasizing the Lord Jesus

Dangerous Territory

For the sake of not unduly loosing anyone too quickly, allow me to discuss the last point first. I have absolutely no problems with Holy Spirit caused, or induced, manifestations. Whether it is Holy Spirit induced laughter, weeping, shaking, or such things as gold dust appearing, or even gold teeth. My concern is rooted in the hunger for these things trumping the hunger and thirst for the person of God and His righteousness. As my friend Loren Sandford has written, "In the church today there is a trend toward seeking ways and means to generate these experiences by our own initiative."

The danger of seeking after spiritual phenomena is really two fold: Firstly, it ends up becoming a downward spiral of deemphasizing the Person and lordship of Christ in one's life and ministry. Secondly, it opens the door for demonic deception in a huge way. The devil can, *and will,* appear as an angel of light if that's what you're hungering for. My fear regarding this current hunger for phenomena is summed up by the apostle Paul's words found in 2 Corinthians 11:3. "I am afraid that, as the serpent deceived Eve by his craftiness, your minds will be led astray from the simplicity and purity *of devotion* to Christ."

Ministries which continually emphasize extreme phenomena and revelation do so to their own, and others, destruction. There is absolutely nothing more extreme than the love, the compassion, the power, and the majesty of God Himself. The moment we begin to emphasize His gifts, or manifestations, more than He, Himself, we are headed down the same track of those carnally obsessed lost souls Paul spoke of in Romans. They chose to exchange the worship of creation for the worship of the Creator!

Until we have truly grasped and realized the height, the width, the depth, and the breadth of God's love let's not settle for focusing on anything less than that. If, as we journey with God, He sovereignly causes phenomena to happen and releases paradigm shaking revelations then let's grow in our sense of amazement and wonder of His goodness. But to digress from seeking Him and not allowing Him to lead us and guide us as He sees fit is a demonic digression.

WHAT'S BEING BUILT- THE KINGDOM OF GOD, OR THE EMPIRES OF MAN?

Earlier this year (I won't say when, or where) I spoke at a conference with two other speakers. One of the speakers took one of the night sessions and spoke 3 hours and mentioned the Lord Jesus twice in passing. The Bible was never once referred to. His whole message, and his whole ministry I suspect, was all about... his ministry. God wants to heal us of all woundedness, but there is such a thing as a Godly brokenness which David sang about in Psalm 51:16, 17 (NASB):

> *You do not delight in sacrifice, otherwise I would give it; You are not pleased with burnt offering. The sacrifices of God are a broken spirit; A broken and a contrite heart, O God, You will not despise.*

This "godly brokenness" of David's is evident in his prayer in Psalm 27:

> *One thing I have asked from the LORD, that I shall seek: That I may dwell in the house of the LORD all the days of my life, To behold the beauty of the LORD And to meditate in His temple.*

Jesus' whole ministry on earth was to restore people to a vital relationship with the Father (John 17:3). His protein, what nourished Him, was to do the will of the Father. He was so fixated on pleasing the Father He walked away when the crowd wanted to crown Him—it simply wasn't the Father's time. Too many ministries today, however, run to any opportunity at all of being crowned before men.

Speaking for myself, I love to tell testimonies of God healing, delivering, and revealing Himself to people. And I thoroughly enjoy the privilege of being able to be part of the process. But there is a huge difference between telling stories in such a way that glorifies the Father, the Son, and the Holy Spirit as opposed to glorifying me, myself, and I. Much of the self-promotion being done today on websites, book covers, and presentations is at the very least self-aggrandizement and at worst demonic in that it, again, deemphasizes the wonder of Jesus. And what seems to be a bigger problem is the willingness of many Charismatics to chase after ministries that are preoccupied with themselves. After nearly sixty years of the countless moral failings of supposed giants of faith with midget-sized character the Charismatic and Pentecostal church is still hungering for the next hero. This speaks volumes of our lack of discernment due to a lack of experience with the real thing—Jesus. At the very least let's take hold of Paul's wisdom regarding reputation: *"For it is not he who commends himself that is approved, but he whom the Lord commends"* (2 Corinthians 10:18). Let's live and breathe for the commendation that comes from God. That commendation is often far from the conference crowd.

DOES TRUTH MATTER?

Two presidencies ago (in the U.S.) the president was caught in a very public lie regarding martial infidelity. At one point while being questioned he responded to a particular question with the question: "what does 'is' mean." Essentially, with one swell swoop the truthful meaning of words was, to a large degree, thrown out the window. And while politicians have always been politic to the point of saying the right things to the right crowd, in today's arena of public speaking, whether political, or otherwise, truth is now largely seen as negotiable. In a demonic Machiavellian manner the end justifies whatever means are utilized.

This almost absolute disregard for truth has, in turn, infected some contemporary ministries. When I speak of prophetic ministry I am more speaking of the ministry of prophets as opposed to the ministry of prophetically gifted people in the local church. These are two very different ministries with two widely differing spheres of influence.

The first red flags I began to notice were back in 1998 and 1999. At that time it was quite fashionable, albeit un-anointed, to prophetically jump on the Y2K bandwagon. A lot of the "whose who" in the prophetic arena prophesied that global economic destruction was going to take place as we entered the new millennium due to the computers not being able to handle the digital change. While I have certainly made my share of prophetic mistakes I heard the Lord say quite clearly that not only was the Y2K catastrophe not going to happen, but the false prophecies were actually going to derail many churches which were quite focused on prayer and outreach to their communities. To a certain degree this did happen. Many churches began to focus on the supposed inspired message to buy generators, store up food, water, and supplies and get ready. Well, the catastrophe never happened. And a lot of the church members who were part of those "get ready for the worst" scenarios ended up very disillusioned with prophetic ministry. I saw first hand how the number of churches in North America, Europe, and the UK who were beginning to grow substantially in intimacy with God and seeking to know His voice began to view current prophecy with real skepticism.

As bad as all of that was, that in and of itself, was not the worst part of the problem. The big problem was the lack of accountability. Very few of the big voices who had given the false words ever came back in a public way and said "sorry." For the most part no one is expecting prophets to be perfectly accurate. We understand the emphasis in the New Covenant is for the hearer of the word to correctly weigh the word and see if it bears witness with his or her own discernment from the Holy Spirit. But to the level that God grants visibility accountability must be in evidence, or else the whole of the ministry comes into disrepute.

A friend of mine who pastors an influential church on the East Coast confronted one of the loudest voices of the Y2K message. When he asked for a mere public acknowledgement of being wrong that prophet responded "oh no, because we prophesied the warning the church prayed and the problem never happened"! The problem with the justification, however, was it was simply dead wrong. The prophecy had not been "if My people pray." It had been "this will absolutely happen and God will use the chaos to birth revival." Now 10 years down the road many so called prophetic ministries use this sort of "open ended" theology as a loop-hole for false prophecies. Any evidence of humility and authentic accountability has been thrown by the wayside. The evidence of this can be seen in the 2008 U.S. presidential elections when so many prophetic ministries cooked up wrong predictions as to who would win. And only a few of those I know of who falsely predicted the outcome have publicly acknowledged their mistake.

In order for the body of Christ to take seriously a critically important God given gift, there must be accountability within the context of grace. Since many prophetic ministers head up their own ministries, the weight is doubly on them to regard grace based accountability as a context for the operation of the gift. Otherwise the gift of God speaking will continue to be devalued in the church at large and those ministries will end up kings of "anointed entertainment." There will be a degree of revelation and power but it will not have the true kingdom fruit God desires.

If we are going to represent the truth of Jesus, in truth, then that begins with our hearts and motives being focused and absorbed with the Truth, Himself. Let's take heed of the prayer from the "man who shook the world": "Now to Him who is able to do far more abundantly beyond all that we ask or think, according to the power that works within us, to Him *be* the glory in the church and in Christ Jesus to all generations forever and ever. Amen."

Marc A. Dupont is the founder of Mantle of Praise Ministries, a ministry concerned with revival and restoring a prophetic edge to the whole body of Christ.

www.marcdupontministries.com

GOD IS PRESENT-FUTURE

by Graham Cooke

Why does God give us prophetic words that can be so far into the future we often feel that we cannot connect with them now? He loves us to have a horizon in our life, something to aim for and head towards in our relationship with Him.

"For I know the plans I have for you, plans for your welfare and not your calamity, to give you a future and a hope" (Jeremiah 29:11). These plans will connect us with our destiny, identity, and calling.

The principle of a future directive word is: The Father puts words long term into our future because He wants to explore them in the Spirit and bring them into our present relationship with Him.

There are two ways that we walk in the natural. Firstly, we look at the ground around our feet so that we do not stumble or step into something nasty. Secondly, we look ahead at where we are going. Our horizon may be limited, but we look for landmarks of note to guide us.

What is true in the natural is also true in the Spirit. We look at where we are now in our fellowship with the Father, and we look ahead to where He is taking us in relationship. It is normal for us to have two perceptions on life; we live today and plan for the future. People who pay conscious attention to the interplay between present and future usually lead successful, productive lives. Those who only live for the moment seldom fulfill their potential and usually live with regret that they had not done enough with their life.

Present-future is also a way of thinking. It is a mentality

that all fruitful people develop. We always make decisions now with the future in mind. We do not want to just move from crisis to crisis. We do not want our future to be a hostage of decisions we make in the present.

This is why meditation and reflection are so vital for us in life. The capacity to pause and calmly think about things (Selah) is an important part of our fellowship with the Holy Spirit, Who is a genius at doing life!

If we really want to be transformed across the whole of our life in fellowship with the Lord, then we must be renewed in how we think (Romans 12:2). "As a man thinks in his heart so is he" (Proverbs 23:7).

What we think about God is the most important thing in life. Too many Christians are trying to have faith without being settled in their hearts about who God is for them and what He is really like in Himself. They have little chance of becoming a man/woman after God's heart because their own heart is not fixed. When our heart is unsure, our head is double-minded.

Our testimony is always concerned not just with what Jesus has done (that's our history), but primarily with who He is for us now. What are we discovering presently about God's nature? What are we exploring about the future in Him? Our present fellowship provides future assurances about our walk with Him. He who began a good work in us will perfect it in Christ Jesus (Philippians 1:6). Paul drew lots of confidence from his present-future way of relating to the Lord.

If what we think about God is most vital, then surely what He thinks about us is just as important. The Father's loving disposition towards us is absolutely essential to our wellbeing, both in the natural and in the Spirit. This revelatory knowledge when combined with actual physical, emotional, mental, and spiritual encounters and experiences of God's nature becomes to us the very evidence of the incarnate

Gospel. We are living proof of Good News!

Our thinking needs adjusting on two levels. Firstly, regarding our ongoing thoughts, ideas, and reasoning about ourselves. Our innermost, heartfelt, emotional perceptions of ourselves must fit the way that God knows us and sees us in Christ.

Secondly, it is absolutely essential that we come to the place of understanding, agreeing with, and consciously aligning ourselves with God's view of us both in the present and with the future. It is much more than an agreed perception; it's the basis of an upgraded relationship!

We see this, most particularly in God's fellowship and relationship with Abraham. In Genesis 18:17-19, we see the Lord visiting Abraham and Sarah. He tells them they will have a son by the next year and Sarah has a fit of the giggles inside the tent. As the Lord is leaving after lunch, He makes this statement about Abraham to the two angels who are traveling with Him: "Shall I hide from Abraham what I am about to do, since Abraham will surely become a great and mighty nation, and in him shall all the nations of the earth will be blessed?"

Firstly, "Shall I hide" really means: I choose to include Abraham. I will open something up to Abraham. I will hear his thoughts. God is taking Abraham into His confidence. This represents an upgrade in their relationship.

Secondly, the most powerful word in this statement is the word "since." God begins a dialogue, which obviously originated in Heaven concerning Abraham and his destiny. "I will include Abraham in what I am doing next...since...(i.e. for the reason that) Abraham will become a great and mighty nation."

It was a done deal in the heart of the Lord. He wanted to connect Abraham's present with his future. The Lord is going to include Abraham in what He is doing now because of what He sees Abraham will become in the future. He lives in the gap between our present and our future, relating to us easily in both contexts. Jesus, who ever lives to make intercession for us (Hebrews 7:25), stands in the gap between our present identity and our future destiny.

God speaks to us prophetically about our future and then relates to us in the present through our destiny. God begins to develop us from the place of our future towards where we are in the present. We partner with the Holy Spirit by cooperating in the present with our future in mind. In this way between our fellowship/relationship we always connect with our present-future.

All success is backwards. When developing a business, we start with a launch date in mind and then work backwards to the present to determine a pathway of development. It is called a critical path analysis that allows us to work out everything that must be accomplished and the order of sequence to ensure a timely launch of our product and resources.

When the Lord speaks prophetically He has a date of fulfillment in mind. After the release of the word He begins to work in our hearts and lives to ensure that the prophetic word comes to pass. When we fail to respond to that process of change and development, then the timing of fulfillment is delayed. Continuous not responding may postpone fulfillment indefinitely and could lead to cancellation.

He works from the future He has declared towards the present that we occupy. What attributes and character traits must I develop in line with the person that He perceives me to become? All discipleship is undertaken with the future in mind, not just the present. God begins with fullness in mind and takes us back to our present lack of resources in order to teach us about faith and provision.

If God has spoken prophetically about us, then we are not living in the present with no concept of our future. We have a God who knows our future and tells us how to align ourselves with Him to create a pathway from now to then and there.

Jesus loved to say, "An hour is coming (future) and even now is (present)" (John 4:23; 5:25; 16:32). The seeds of that hour to come are in the present with us now! The fruit of that future time will be realized if we nurture the seed that is currently present. God sees the end from the beginning and is always in both places at once. Which is precisely the reason why we can always know rest and peace.

He plans our journey by His own desire to be present with us! He is so trustworthy in this regard.

The LORD your God who goes before you will Himself fight on your behalf, just as He did for you in Egypt before your eyes, and in the wilderness where you saw how the LORD your God carried you, just as a man carries his son, in all the way which you have walked until you came to this place. But for all this, you did not trust the LORD your God, who goes before you on your way, to seek out a place for you to encamp, in fire by night and cloud by day, to show you the way in which you should go. (Deuteronomy 1:30-33)

He goes before us. He carries us through the difficult times. He seeks out a place for us to inhabit and He shows us the way. He is fully present-future with His people. Prophecy connects our present with His future. He speaks to us from our future and works to develop us today so that we can become aligned with our truest identity as He perceives it. We then have the pleasure of cooperating and moving towards the future with the Holy Spirit.

Prophecy begins a process; a series of steps that will take us to our destiny. It is vital that we align ourselves with the process, rather than just the destiny. Many people want the outcome but not the journey of transformation. The process is concerned with establishing our identity. The outcome is focused on achieving destiny. No identity, no destiny. There is no future without process. It is the process that makes us rich.

Because He sees our potential for destiny and then

speaks it to us, God begins to deal with us from the viewpoint of destiny perceived rather than destiny pronounced. Personal prophecy relates more to the possibility rather than the inevitability of fulfillment. All personal prophecy is conditional upon response and obedience.

The purpose of development time is to enable us to work with the Holy Spirit so that our prophetic future can become a present reality. Our prophetic word describes our next piece of territory whether it is relational, personal, or ministerial. We have to go there, explore it, and bring into the present the attitude and persona required to respond, take ground, and inherit the promise.

Israel had received prophetic promises regarding Canaan. They sent out a group of men (the best warrior in each tribe) to explore the territory and bring back a report (Numbers chapters 13-14). Only Joshua and Caleb had a right attitude towards what God had promised. They looked at Canaan in the light of God's nature and His prophetic promise. They saw nothing in the land that would prevent them from inheriting it. They realized all along that the fulfillment of prophecy depends upon alignment with God, not our own capacity to perform. Read their report:

Then Moses and Aaron fell on their faces in the presence of all the assembly of the congregation of the sons of Israel. Joshua the son of Nun and Caleb the son of Jephunneh, of those who had spied out the land, tore their clothes; and they spoke to all the congregation of the sons of Israel, saying, "The land which we passed through to spy out is an exceedingly good land. If the LORD is pleased with us, then He will bring us into this land and give it to us—a land which flows with milk and honey. Only do not rebel against the LORD; and do not fear the people of the land, for they will be our prey. Their protection has been removed from them, and the LORD is with us; do not fear them." (Numbers 14:5-9)

Alignment is only about pleasing the Lord.

Development is about becoming the people that God perceives; turning potential into something actual. At the very least, do not rebel against God, and do not fear the opposition. Process is about experiencing the effect of God's favor. They shall be our prey. Their protection is removed. God is with us! Process is about developing confidence in God's name, nature, and intentionality.

Joshua and Caleb explored the territory that God promised. They brought back courage, confidence, and faith. They became a stakeholder in their own future. All success is backward. We must be in agreement with the end result before we start. When God shows us the finished article that He sees when He looks at us, we must take hold of that in our heart. Create a link between the person we are now and the one described in the prophecy.

When Moses was sent to Egypt to speak to Pharaoh and demand the release of Israel, understandably he had some misgivings about himself (Exodus chapters 4-6). He had many excuses and fears that caused his sense of inadequacy to be almost tangible. The only antidote to our lack of vision is the one that God is seeing when He looks at us!

"See, I have made you as God to Pharaoh, and your brother, Aaron, shall be your prophet" (Exodus 7:1). God sets markers down on our horizon. To fulfill that word we must develop a greater spiritual dimension in and around ourselves, particularly so that we can encounter and experience faith, favor, intimacy, and authority. If Moses does not see himself the way that God does there is no possibility of him traveling to Egypt. If he does not agree and align himself with God's view of him, then he cannot generate enough faith to overcome his own fear. If he does not take on the characteristics of faith, power, and authority, he cannot stand before Pharaoh. He must become the Deliverer in his heart before he steps into Egypt.

This is a Scriptural principle not just a prophetic

precept. Paul expounded it in Philippians 3:12-17:

> *Not that I have already obtained it or have already become perfect,*
> *but I press on so that I may lay hold of that for which also I was*
> *laid hold of by Christ Jesus. Brethren, I do not regard myself as*
> *having laid hold of it yet; but one thing I do: forgetting what lies*
> *behind and reaching forward to what lies ahead, I press on toward*
> *the goal for the prize of the upward call of God in Christ Jesus.*
> *Let us therefore, as many as are perfect, have this attitude; and if in*
> *anything you have a different attitude, God will reveal that also to*
> *you; however, let us keep living by that same standard to which we*
> *have attained. Brethren, join in following my example, and observe*
> *those who walk according to the pattern you have in us.*

We are either enjoying our possession or actively pressing in to take it. The language here makes a powerful statement of intent. "I press on, in order to take hold." Real believers will always believe! They are honest, and they have a plan. "I am not there yet, but my strategy is to forget the past and reach out for my future." There is a pattern of behavior in faith that enables us to reach our destiny more quickly. It involves being present-future and not present-past in our outlook on life.

God speaks from the place of your future completion into the place of your present fullness. Take it on board. We can live from the past into our present and be undone by prior circumstances, or we can live from the future into our present and be edified by God's view of our real identity. But we cannot do both without destroying our momentum.

Our destiny does not come to meet us; we reach out for it and press towards it. We attract it to us by how we live our faith. We are learning to be as intentional about our future as the Lord is about our life in Christ in the present.

Prophecy promotes who we are in the Spirit. We learn confidence in that identity and God's intent. We develop the mindset, character, and attributes that are in line with God's frame of reference. That mindset includes all the possibilities of ongoing victory. Whatever is going to oppose us on this level is smaller than God's perception of us.

"We can do all things through Christ who strengthens us" (Philippians 4:13). This is a mindset! A mindset dominates our personality so that we become that mentally, emotionally, and physically. The viewpoint of God towards us will release favor as we partner with Him, Rise up, take possession of identity and destiny. Own it. Wear it. Become involved with it!

Our favor attracts faith. We will need an upgraded provision of this new level of identity. This will be contested by the enemy who must surely be worried about a present-future disposition. He controls us when we live present-past, but has no authority when we press into the prophetic. We need a mindset that can receive under pressure. Crucially, our future self has never known defeat. Prophecy is history spoken and written in advance. In our mindset we must develop our identity from the place of advancement (future) and bring it into the present.

The crucial questions are:

- What is the difference between where we are now and where we need to go?
- What must change in our relationship with God and how we connect with Him in this new season of His will for us?
- What must change in our personality as we pursue this mindset?

We have been present-past in our life for far too long. It is time to forget what lies behind and reach out to what is before us. If we are to really become significant people, we must live a prophetic lifestyle. We are present-future in Christ.

Graham Cooke is a popular conference speaker and is well known for his training programs on the prophetic, spiritual warfare and intimacy with God, leadership and spirituality.

www.grahamcooke.com

CRYPTIC WARNINGS & WHAT, ME WORRY?

by Julia Loren

What do you do with the things God shows you or words spoken by the prophets of our time – especially in this international climate of fear and uncertainty that pervades the media and unsettles our hearts?

During the morning church service on the first Sunday in January 2001, the pastor of the church I attended invited those who felt like they had prophetic words about the coming year to stand and speak. So, I stood up and said, "I had a dream of a stealth aircraft carrier coming into San Diego harbor. I believe that by the end of the year our nation will be at war." It wasn't a very Happy New Year prophetic word and no one knew what to do with that word. No one realized how the church could be impacted by such an event, nor did they focus on gearing up for an outreach to the young Marines and their families stationed at a nearby base.

A few months later, I stood worshipping the Lord during a conference held in Kansas City. Suddenly, a many-winged creature flew into view from my left hand side. It drew a six-foot wide curtain across the front of the platform, near where I stood. Another creature took up the opposite edge and they hovered in front of me, as the curtain became a private big screen TV. I wanted to stare at the creatures that defied description but the movie began and caught my attention as footage of horrible scenes emerged. From an aerial view, I saw a crowd of high school students running, scattering out of the line of fire. The scene followed one student in particular who looked like he had been shot. Then the scene changed to a city street. Tall buildings, narrow streets, people running terrified as a cloud of ashy substance chased them. Some were pulled to safety inside other buildings. It wasn't smoke. It was more like buildings collapsing rapidly behind them. It seemed as if an earthquake was centered only in one area of the city and I knew it was bad.

Suddenly, the screen and creatures disappeared and I found myself on my knees weeping, stunned. Later that night, I told my friend and traveling companion what I had seen and said, "I am going home to a major school shooting that will happen probably on Monday. And what follows that will be even worse." It was Saturday when I saw the vision. On Monday, I sat in a management meeting in the school principal's office where I was working as a counselor when the secretary interrupted our meeting with the announcement of a school shooting that was occurring at Santana High School, in our San Diego school district. I had watched the actual news footage shown on the TV in the Spirit that I would see on the TV at the school 48 hours later.

By September, the second half of the news footage unfolded as I watched the rubble and dust cloud chase terrified people down the streets of New York. We knew our nation was going to war that day. And I spent the next week counseling students and staff at the schools we had on the local military base.

I hate many of the dreams and visions I receive because of the traumatizing impact they have on me but I know enough to ask, *What am I supposed to do with the things you show me, Lord?*

How we perceive the nature of God dictates our response to the things He shows us. If we see Him as loving and kind, we will reach out in compassion, extending His peace and healing to all who are in need—believers and non-believers alike. If we see Him as judgmental and vengeful, we will sit back and do nothing, or act only on behalf of our families and those we love.

I felt the Holy Spirit tell me that 2001 was the beginning of a new era and that I should obtain the credentials I needed to be able to walk onto any disaster site or any US military base around the world and be an agent of peace and healing. True to God's word, He backed it up with the divine appointments and connections that I needed to obtain the credentials to extend His presence and love to others. I was being called to step up and use my credentials in ways I never expected. That season lasted until recently.

So what do you do with the things God shows you? Or the prophecies that God reveals to others?

Throughout history, God spoke to His prophets about times to come, often through visions of doom and gloom. He gave Daniel visions that actually traumatized him. These visions were so graphic in detail about the future of the world that afterwards, an overwhelmed Daniel took to his bed and cried out in intercession asking for an increase in understanding the days that God revealed. Other prophets cried out and asked God to stay His hand after they heard or saw what was to occur in the days to come. The apostle John also saw troubling visions about the end of days, days that some people believe are upon us now.

PROPHETS OF DOOM OR PROPHETS OF HOPE?

Although you may not see the Biblical prophets who speak of doom and gloom as "prophets of hope", they can be. It depends on how you interpret their words. God's words release hope if you hear the word of wisdom hidden behind each word and understand how you are personally called to respond. When people gather together and hear a word that sounds like doom and gloom, everyone responds differently. Some only hear the gloom. Others see the glory about to unfold.

Word got around one particular city that a meeting would be held at a certain believer's house—a meeting you wouldn't want to miss that would certainly encourage the ever-growing ranks of Greeks in Antioch who had become followers of Jesus. They were becoming known as "Christians", the latest fad to hit the religious scene, a fad that turned its backs on centuries of Greek god and goddess worship for a single man who was said to have raised himself from the dead and releases spiritual gifts. They called their gifted oracles "prophets". Several of them had arrived from Jerusalem and the meeting in Antioch would be amazing.

Who knows how many gathered that night? Some sat on the floor with their eyes wide open taking in the scene, while others sat with their heads bowed, listening, praying, their spiritual senses heightened by the Presence in the room, the air pulsing with the energy of the Holy Spirit combined with their anticipation. Surely God was about to speak. One of the men, known for hearing accurately about times to come, a man named Agabus, broke the tension as he stood and began to speak. Through the Spirit, he predicted that a severe famine would spread through the entire Roman world. (Acts 11:25-30)

The Presence of God (the Holy Spirit) filled the room and touched each listener's heart as if whispering, "Listen, this prophet is speaking a word that could only come by revelation from me. What he is saying is true." And so they listened and talked among themselves about what a famine would mean to them and to their brothers and sisters in the region that would be most impacted.

Their response turned a gloomy prophetic word about an impending disaster away from being a word of judgment and transformed it into a word of hope and redemption.

Imagine with me, for a moment, what those men listening to Agabus immediately thought. I imagine that one man thought, "What does this famine have to do with me? Famines happen all the time. My family will be unaffected so why should I be concerned? God helps those who help themselves."

Yet another likely thought, "It is the judgment of God upon them. Everyone knows their ruler Claudius is corrupt in thought and deed and hates the Jews. Who can avert God's judgment and why should we? They need to repent. The rain falls on the just and the unjust alike."

Another perhaps thought, "The tenderness of Jesus caused Him to reach out to feed the poor and heal the sick, so this is certainly not His will that people should perish. If they were my family, I'd want to make sure they were well protected. This is a wakeup call for me to become prepared for the outbreak of famine, war, emergencies, and disasters that could occur in my area and reach out to others during times of need."

One individual likely immediately strategized about what to do. "Jesus was certainly a practical prophet. He took loaves and fishes from a little boy and multiplied the food source. We could take what little we have and send it to them. We should send our fellow believers, our brothers and sisters in Christ, some money to build up their food supply while the community is still selling commodities. We have very little time. If the famine happens next year, they need to buy during this harvest season."

A businessman in the room probably thought, "How can I use this information to invest wisely so that I can help secure the future of my family for the coming generations, my community, and wherever else God calls me to give to the body of Christ in the future? Jesus spoke about the "talents", investing wisely to multiply the resources and that He gives us. Surely, He will grant me wisdom to create wealth and like Joseph, have the foresight to store up those resources and dispense them in the future."

As they talked among themselves, the word of wisdom came through consensus and they decided that a collection must be taken and sent to the region through a trusted envoy. Who better than Barnabus and Saul to deliver both the money and impress upon them the reason for the gift?

That night, several things became clear: God is not the God who wills disaster, but a God who provides before the disaster even happens because God knows when it is about to occur. God knows how to meet the needs of His people before they even know they are needy! And God continues to speak through His prophets. The prophetic word of doom became an avenue of hope and redemption for many whose lives and livelihoods were saved because true listeners are not just titillated by words from God, they take it to prayer and community and seek God for how they should respond. Those who knew the true nature of God—that God is love—responded in love and action.

It takes a listening community who is tuned into His voice and has taken stock of the resources and which individual among them carries what specific spiritual and natural gifts. And it takes a word of wisdom to know what to do with the things that you hear.

But what if...those listening to the prophet's word simply stood up and appealed to the God of Love and used their authority to stop the famine through prayer? We respond according to the level of our faith and how we perceive the Lord. The same Holy Spirit resides in us as it did in Jesus. When Jesus stood up in the boat and rebuked the wind and the waves, who was He rebuking? The enemy and his plans for destruction. Are we not filled with the same power and authority? Or do we believe that things are already set in motion and are fixed to a cosmic timeline so we cannot calm the storms, divert the winds, or stop the raging seas and erupting volcanoes? Who are we colluding with—the plans of the evil one who is hell bent on destruction, or the plans of the

Lord for total redemption and healing of the peoples and the lands of our global home?

Let's go back to those fictitious men who I imagine listened to the prophet's word about the famine. The first man failed to listen, failed to prepare, and his heart was more focused on himself than filled with compassion and wisdom. God only knows what happened to him. The second thought God's will was to judge and let them all perish. The third prepared an emergency food supply and disaster plan for his family in case they might have to flee from some future disaster. His heart felt peaceful because he knew that he was prepared. Another man developed a response and recovery plan that enabled whole communities to mobilize and reach out in the love and compassion of God to others who would be impacted. Hundreds and thousands of people came to know the love of Jesus and enter into the salvation of Christ because of his outreach. The last man, the businessman, knowing that food prices would rise as energy costs soared, invested in the stock market, made a fortune off misfortune, and reinvested the earnings into companies that would mitigate against future losses for entire communities and minimize damage. He acted not just to enrich himself or to assist only fellow believers. He used his investment for all humankind, including those who had no faith in any God, because he was filled with the love and wisdom of God who cares for all of Creation. He also knew that crisis meant opportunity and he shifted his emotions and thoughts into productive avenues and action. But perhaps one man, Paul or Barnabus or an unknown new believer, could have stood up and said, "No" to the famine and averted disaster.

Now, come with me out of the book of Acts and into New Orleans, Louisiana in August 2005. I was there, in the aftermath. Just like the men in Antioch who heard the word of an impending natural disaster, people responded differently to the prophetic words God released to many prophets before the hurricane ever hit.

Many Christians heard or read the words of well-known Christian prophets who predicted a storm would hit New Orleans. A couple of prophets "saw" New Orleans underwater, predicting the levies would fail. One Baton Rouge pastor told me that prophet Bob Jones said that his church would become the epicenter of recovery after New Orleans was flooded—long before Hurricane Katrina. His word helped prepare that pastor and his congregation to willingly turn their buildings into a response and recovery center hosting thousands of volunteers from around the nation.

Some Christians said the hurricane was God's judgment. Others said it was the natural consequence of ordinary cycles of hurricanes complicated by poor building planning and bad planning regarding levy safety. Still others, who had heard the warnings, watched in horror and knew that they were being prompted by the Love of God to suspend judgment and act in compassion—for their God is a God of Love and compassion. Businessmen mobilized and rushed around frantically trying to discover the right state and federal contacts who could tell them how they might obtain contracts from the government for the response and recovery efforts. Those businesses that had prepared beforehand already had the FEMA contacts and contracts ready to sign and were prepared to prosper. Pastors stepped up and turned their buildings into shelters and feeding stations. Some opened their buildings to volunteers from around the world who descended on the area with chain saws and practical tools to assist with the recovery. The racial divide was closed for a season as blacks helped whites and whites helped blacks in the initial aftermath.

Hurricane Katrina woke us all up and called us all to respond in some way and our responses revealed what was in our own hearts—judgment, apathy, greed or love—and how much we reflected the nature of Jesus.

As for the people of New Orleans, most of them never

heard the words of the prophets predicting what was going to happen months before Hurricane Katrina hit. Most did not have the means or preparation to leave New Orleans and so they suffered or lost their lives. A few prepared. One woman I met had gathered a stash of cash and prepared an evacuation plan because she wanted to ensure not just her own safety, but the safety of her children and grandchildren. She gathered them all and fled ahead of the storm as far north as she could. Some failed to listen to the warnings about the strength of the storm. Others never heard the prophetic words that went beyond the newscasts—words that spoke of New Orleans being under water. It should have been a clue that the only way that could happen was for levies to fail. Had the prophets been given a louder voice in the city, had their words been more respected, more lives could have been spared and the response and recovery time greatly improved.

What do we do with what prophets speak? I believe we should do what they did in Antioch...listen as a community and seek God for how we should respond, not just as individuals, but also as a community of believers—even for the sake of unbelievers.

We all hear imperfectly. We all have the same Holy Spirit speaking and yet each one of us interprets what we hear differently. That is why we need to dwell in a community of listeners, who can bring their different ways of thinking and different interpretations to the table and listen for the true interpretation of the word of the Lord, and more importantly, what God is calling them to do with that word.

Within 40 years, the coming generation will see a world-wide population explosion that will tax all of our resources. Every natural, technological, or man-made disaster will impact a huge population. It will become more important than ever before to develop community, where people trust one another, where every individual has developed the ability to draw close to the Lord and listen intently and accurately for the word that He speaks. We will need to listen not just for ourselves, but also for one another, as never before.

In a sense, we must all become prophets—those who listen, those who receive revelation directly from the throne of heaven, and have the history of relationships and accuracy in revelation so well-developed that others trust them. They have earned that trust because they have the integrity to not lead others astray with their visions, their dream interpretations, or their revelations. We must become prophets to the unbelievers who seek revelation in non-Christian sources— the psychics, astrologers, and shamans—and release the truth of God's Presence, power, and wisdom as we step out in love and compassion.

When you hear or read a prophet's word, listen for the message of hope hidden in the word. What is God calling you to do with that word? How should you respond? Consider these words as if God is speaking directly to you. Most words may not resonate with you. But suddenly, as you read or hear one spoken, one will leap off the page and pierce your heart. You will know it because you will want to read it over and over. Take that as a sign that God is speaking to you through that word. Seek Him for how you can respond and draw out the message of hope and release it to others.

You have a unique way of seeing and perceiving the world. You also have a specific mix of natural and spiritual gifts that you carry within you. Ask God to show you those gifts within you and the gift that you are to the world in this hour of history. You are purposed to be here for such a time as this. God knows the times and seasons in which you live. God created you and longs for a relationship with you and desires to give you revelation of your purpose and future. Take time to interact with the Holy Spirit in these days ahead, and ask God questions. He hears your spoken and unspoken thoughts. Ask for divine appointments and strategy to reach your destiny as you do your own listening. Draw closer to God. Let's move deeper and higher into His presence rather than run away and hide in fear and self-absorption. Let's all become messengers of hope to a crazy world.

PROPHETS REVEAL THE TRUE NATURE OF GOD

God's ways are not our ways. He is not the author of confusion (1 Corinthians 14:33). He is one whose perfect love casts out fear —He doesn't cause it (1 John 4:18). His plan is to give us a future and a hope—no matter what happens in the earth (Proverbs 23:18 & Jeremiah 29:11). He sends His word to encourage us, to comfort us, and to prepare us for the days ahead. He doesn't send His word to judge us—for Christ came not to condemn the world but to save it (John 3:17). He sends His word to turn our hearts towards Him—not to scare the hell out of us and cause us to think He is evil in His intent towards us. Any words or thoughts in your head about anything other than the supreme goodness of God are twisted lies. True prophets and true followers of Christ know the personality and nature of Christ. They know that God does not will that any should perish but that all should be redeemed. Jesus is in the seek-and-save business, not the condemn-and-annihilate business.

True prophets may speak words of doom and gloom— but they are spoken with redemption in mind or to prepare you and encourage you to interact with God about how you should respond. True prophets also speak about the glory to be revealed in and through you. They talk about the Church, what it is going to look like and how it will function in a seemingly post-Christian world. Most of all, they reveal the nature of God the Father, Jesus the Savior, and the Holy Spirit who is the very real Presence of God on earth, our comforter, our counselor.

Do you really know much about the goodness of God and can you access His Presence during these stressful days we live in? True prophets will help lead you in and lift you higher.

God is not out to frighten or manipulate you and press you into some mold that conforms to archaic religion. True prophets will lead you to see the goodness of God through the understanding that warnings are about redemption, and that God has called you to be His most loved, special friend, one whom He trusts and confides in, and one whom you can trust and confide in as well. You can walk confidently into the future with Jesus saying, "How kind He is! How good He is! So gracious towards me and full of compassion! So merciful this God of ours!" (Psalm 116)

I want to leave you with one final thought:

The abundant life is about living in the presence of God. During these days ahead, hold onto who God really is: God is Love & God is Good. Inhale His love and exhale His peace. Center yourself there.

Julia Loren is the author of several books including: *Shifting Shadows of Supernatural Power, Shifting Shadows of Supernatural Experiences, Supernatural Anointing, When God Says Yes, & Divine Intervention: True Stories of Heaven Invading Earth.*
www.divineinterventionbooks.com

The

Wonders

Beyond 2012

THE LIGHT & THE DARKNESS

by James Maloney

Arise, shine; for your light has come! And the glory of the Lord is risen upon you. For behold, the darkness shall cover the earth, and deep darkness the people; but the Lord will arise over you, and His glory will be seen upon you. The Gentiles shall come to your light, and kings to the brightness of your rising. (Isaiah 60:1-3)

I believe the Lord has shown, that if Jesus should tarry, let's say, another thirty years, the body of Christ will spiritually fulfill Isaiah Chapters 60-66. It is my firm persuasion that we are coming into Chapter 60 right now, and this period will last several years with an overlap of the continuing chapters, phasing in at different intervals of time.

No one can deny there is gross darkness covering the face of the earth. Just in the last fifty years we are seeing a marked increase in violence, apathy, and self-destruction in this country alone. Like the author stated when I was approached to contribute to this book, "Fear is at an all time high." People are desperate for a true touch of God's glory, to demonstrate the reality of Kingdom principles on this earth. Anyone who knows the ministry the Lord has entrusted to me knows I make no pretext for a dynamic need of signs, wonders, and miracles that validate the truth established in God's Word.

The prophetic Spirit has laid upon our hearts a key to recognize the release of this miraculous demonstration through His believers; one that is found in the understanding that the dwelling place (the temple) of God is established already inside each born-again disciple, that we are, indeed, the temple of the Holy Ghost (1 Corinthians 6:19). As such, the spiritual Kingdom of Jesus is already on earth, in us—not just a third heaven experience that must be brought down to this plane of existence. Don't misunderstand. I completely agree with and profess the need of establishing what is in heaven on earth, but let us not forget that we already have the heavenly Kingdom residing in our very spirits. The distinction is slight, yet profound. This Kingdom experience is found not so much in bringing God down to earth (although there is truth in this notion), but in us coming up higher, to His domain, seeking Him at His gates. I sometimes humorously feel that the Lord is tired of always coming down to visit us—why don't we come up to Him? (I'm speaking somewhat facetiously, but the point is valid.) The question becomes: how is this accomplished?

I believe there is an application of Matthew 6:4 that employs more than just "charitable deeds" for what "your Father who sees in secret will Himself reward you openly"— this is a principle of Kingdom release. Coming into that secret place, that inner sanctum, the proverbial "prayer closet," to seek Him in secret, so that He may reward us openly: through the demonstration of His Kingdom come now on earth. It is in this secret place that we are entrusted with Kingdom authority, wisdom and power.

(As an aside, let me then share the importance of Jude 20. As I believe in miraculous demonstration, I also believe in the importance of tongues. Entire segments of Pentecostal or charismatic congregations have moved toward a lessening of the use of praying in tongues — this alarms me! Praying in the Holy Spirit is vital to the building up of our most holy faith and keeping us in the love of God. As we pray in tongues, the Spirit moves us from the soulish realm to the spiritual realm. We come into the holy of holies; there is a cleansing of the soulish debris, the weights and discouragements of life, that inhibit the flow of God's grace in manifestation. Praying in tongues purifies our soulish life. We look forward to the coming of our Lord. As we seek Him in the secret place, the hardened, fallow ground of our souls is plowed and turned up, so the seed sown can germinate in the light and water of the Lord and His Word. It is the release of our heavenly prayer language in that secret place that adds the fresh oil, the anointing, the representation of God's glory, to our light — the Kingdom within us. Without it, we may miss the time of visitation, dear friends!)

I feel the Lord is calling us into an intense time of secret meetings, communicating with Him in the Spirit, so that our light might shine in the darkness in a way before unseen on the earth.

Some would call this a Third Great Awakening. Perhaps that is a good term, because I believe the Lord has revealed through His prophets that entire communities, perhaps entire ethnic groups, will be swept into the Kingdom before His second coming. But I also remind the reader of what Kenneth Hagin, Sr., proclaimed the Lord told him during his time in heaven: that there will also be entire communities, areas of the world, that will not experience another time of awakening because they already missed their time of visitation. (Luke 19:41-44) But don't fear because Jesus said there is always a remnant.

That's us. We are that remnant bringing the light to the darkness. Don't despair! Be prepared.

Twenty-five years ago I believe the Lord told me that starting in 2015 this darkness of Isaiah 60 would begin to increase exponentially across the globe, but that we as the remnant were to arise and shine because the glory of the Lord was risen upon us. This darkness isn't comprised solely of arrant sin, but of a spirit of antichrist. I define a spirit of antichrist as anything that is anti-anointing (Christ means "Anointed One.") Just as Hebrews 13:8-9 proclaims it is a strange and variant doctrine (of a demon, let's be honest) to teach that Jesus Christ is not the same yesterday, today and forever; those who adamantly oppose a doctrine that shows Jesus today operating as He did in Acts 10:38 (see, He was anointed); those who maintain a distinction between Christ and His body in the way we are to operate; those who purport the Holy Spirit has stopped the anointing in this age of cessation; those who claim acts of the supernatural are rooted in evil — these fall dangerously close to blasphemy against that same Spirit who anointed the Christ (Luke 4:14) and anoints His people. (Acts 6:8; 1 Corinthians 12; James 5:14-15) This is the darkness that our light is to overcome.

The ultimate fulfillment of the Lord's prayer in Matthew 6 comes from His people recognizing His Kingdom is come now (check out the original Aramaic) — on earth as it was already being done in heaven. How is this recognized? In letting our light shine — that Light from heaven being experienced in holiness through us — overcoming the deep darkness with the complete representation of Christ's earthly ministry through His body in the same signs, wonders and miracles that He wrought as the God-Man on earth. Yes, we are facing deep darkness, but the Light of the world shining through us will draw the nations.

Conversely with the anti-anointing, after the progression of Isaiah 60, the coming years will see a marked increase in the false anointing, a gift mixture that is pseudo-spiritual, or preternatural, in manifestation, similar to the lying signs and wonders Paul was talking about in 2 Thessalonians 2:9.

Alongside the spiritual fulfillment of Isaiah 60, starting 2015, I believe the Lord has said the strong delusion (2 Thessalonians 2:11; paralleled to Isaiah 66:4 — actually both chapters in their entirety) will begin; people given over to a reprobate mind, believing the lie (Romans 1:25), beginning what Paul proclaimed as the great falling away, the apostasy, leading to the release of the son of perdition. Not so much that believers out-and-out reject salvation, but rather they love not the truth and take pleasure in unrighteousness; they ignore the unadulterated, sound Christian doctrine — the simplicity of Christ, and by association, His anointing. (2 Corinthians 11:3) But don't be fearful — this is not you! Some will fall away from the faith (1 Timothy 4:1) — not you! In the midst of this, I believe the Lord has said He will sanctify His name among His people, and that remnant of which we will be a part shall rise up in a true manifestation of His grace — our staffs will swallow theirs. (Exodus 7:12) It is my personal opinion this is what Zechariah 13:7-10 speaks of — the (comparatively) one-third calls on the name of the Lord. Sadly, it is the two-thirds (again, comparatively) that Paul is speaking about in 2 Thessalonians. However, we — the third — shall withstand the strong delusion, as we draw into the secret place, manifesting the truth of God's word through legitimately delegated authority, power and wisdom in genuine signs, wonders and miracles.

This year, 2011, I believe a divine shift is starting to occur in the Spirit that is leading us into Isaiah 60 and beyond. Primarily, I see this shift stirring the young at heart, those approximately between the ages of eight and sixteen. It is becoming their heart's cry to see the reality of Christ's Kingdom on earth — that manifestation of glory. These young ones are coming into the secret place, being birthed of a quickening anointing that hastens their progression through the Benjamin Gate (see Zechariah 14; Nehemiah 3) — space fails me to elaborate fully on this concept, but reference Genesis 35:18. The "son of my sorrow" is being renamed the "son of my right hand" (the representation of authority and power.) What that means is, for parents out there who have had a hard time instilling your faith into your children, this season is showing a extraordinary hastening of the Lord's work in this younger generation. Maintain your faith; don't waver in your pursuit of a supernatural release of God's glory;

it will prosper in you and your children. It has to! The hearts of the children must be turned to the fathers, and vice versa, lest the earth is smitten with a curse! (Malachi 4:6)

All right, let's wind this down. I believe we will be in the spiritual fulfillment of Isaiah 60 for the next several years, with some overlap of Isaiah 61-66, each chapter phasing in with spiritual application. Starting 2015, there will be an acceleration of the Lord lifting of His hand that restrains the strong delusion. The next several years will be a period of deep darkness, full of continual upheaval and turmoil on a global scale (we're already seeing the rumblings of it now). Be not troubled. (Matthew 24:3-31) There must be wars and rumors of wars, earthquakes and pestilences, leading up to the Great Tribulation and the abomination of desolation.

But don't think I'm sharing doom and gloom. Far from it! If there is darkness, there is light, and it will overcome. In the midst of this great havoc, these next ten to twelve years are going to show a time of unprecedented financial prosperity to this remnant (see Isaiah 60:5), in order that they might get out "this" gospel (Matthew 24:14) — the gospel of the Kingdom of Light: the signs, wonders and miracles that attest to the validity of Christ's true reign — the Lord declares "this" gospel will be preached. (Of course, this great wealth transfer also paves the way secularly for a future one-world monetary system rooted in the European Theatre after the collapse of a time of prosperity, leading eventually into the beginning of sorrows.)

We will see a dismantling of Muslim nations over this time period, similar occurrences to the Berlin Wall, the Iron Curtain, etc. Each of these doors will be opened for just a short period of time for the Light to be preached. But after this season we will see the Pan-Arab nations re-solidify (aligning with China and Russia), turning their sights against natural Israel, heralding the beginning of the end.

I won't be so presumptuous to assume "the end," but

what I wish to delineate and drive home to you, dear reader: the time has come; arise and shine! Let your light pour forth to destroy the darkness.

Just as John declared (John 1:1-5), we have the Life within us, the Light to all man: He will shine in the darkness, and the darkness will by no means overcome. Enter into the inner sanctum of the secret place, build yourselves up in the Spirit, let the Lord's Prayer be your heartbeat of desire. Shine on, my friends!

James Maloney, D.D., Th.D, Ph.D. is President, The ACTS Group International and the author of The Dancing Hand of God; The Wounded Cry; and Aletheia Eleutheroo (forthcoming)
www.answeringthecry.com

URGENT WORDS OF DISASTERS TO COME

by Julia Loren

I've known many ordinary believers who experienced extraordinary dreams, visions, and angelic visitations that spoke of events about to unfold throughout the nations. Maybe you are one who has heard extraordinary things from heaven—or even in a vision of heaven. Some of the people I know had predictive dreams or visions that were accurate. Others were not. My own visions and dreams only release partial information. I once saw a vision of a major school shooting that morphed into the cloud of airborne debris that rolled down city streets terrifying the people who ran ahead of it. I predicted the general area of the school shooting, immediately discerning that it would take place in the school district I was working in that year. But I had no clue that the rest of the vision was about September 11th. I was given no details as to the location, the event, or the date. In fact, I could have interpreted the scene of airborne debris as ash from a volcano, smoke from a fire, or even a nuclear bomb. All I wanted to do was put the image out of my mind—especially after attending to the aftermath of the school shooting at Santana High School that spring.

Years later, in a dream, I received the date December 26 and "saw" that a major disaster would expose much of the child sex slave industry and would be broadcast on Oprah's show for months. The Indonesia and Thailand tsunami occurred on that date and Oprah's show broadcast exactly what I "saw" that she would do in the dream. But I didn't know the exact country or the type of disaster that would happen.

I also saw in another dream, the "royal flush" of leaders out of Arab nations—the "Arab Spring", a few years before it unfolded. But, again, I had no idea of the timing. I only saw in part. As we all do.

Prophets see in part and hear in part. No one knows the whole truth about what is about to occur in the future. We hear bits and pieces. And then it takes years to decipher the language of heaven, the ways God speaks to us individually, through dreams, visions, and angelic visitation. Some dreams are more literal while most are simply symbolic. Some visions can be the product of our own imaginations. Some angels that seem like they are from God may be imposters appearing as angels of light—when in fact, they are sent from Lucifer's camp. No matter how long we have walked with God, we can still be deceived by our own soul or deceived by the enemy. No one is immune. Everything must be tested and discernment is the key to understanding spiritual experiences.

As you read the following prophetic words, read with prayerful discernment. I have purposely edited out most of the statements regarding end times theology or people's opinions about why God would "send" disaster or "warn" of disasters—except for one prediction by Bob Jones that he ties to our nation's influence with Israel. I include that because the Church has yet to shake off replacement theology and wake up to the significance of Israel and why we are called to "pray for the peace of Jerusalem" (Psalm 122:6). We are living in a cosmic timetable of events stated in scripture and revealed on earth in many ways. But no man knows the hour or the day of Christ's return, if it is a literal return or not, if Christians will be taken to heaven (rapture) before world events get really ugly or be spared in the midst of the events. There are so many ways to interpret the end times that it is best to just focus on the words and leave the reasons behind them as big a mystery as the mystery of God's ways and thoughts.

God prepares us ahead of time—regardless of our

theology—to prepare and respond, not just be titillated by the predictions of disasters to come. And it doesn't always take a prophet to warn us. Major quakes strike with alarming regularity: earthquakes of magnitude 7 or greater occur approximately 18 times a year worldwide. They usually originate near faults where tectonic plates —tremendous fragments of the earth's crust—collide or push above or below each other. Scientists believe the potential for the next magnitude 8-9 earthquake striking in 2012 and the decade to come is highest for the following countries: Southern Italy, China, Central Mexico, Tokyo, Japan, Pakistan, Iran, and Indonesia. In the U.S., areas most likely to be impacted by earthquakes are along the Hayward or San Andreas faults in California, the New Madrid fault line in southeastern Missouri, and the Cascadia subduction zone located 50 miles off the coast of Oregon, Washington, and southern British Columbia.

Most natural disasters occur seasonally. Tornados strike the mid-west every April and May. 2011 was the fourth deadliest tornado year in U.S. history. Hurricanes and cyclones whirl in from the sea every year as well—some years are deadlier than others. While scientists can predict the severity of a tornado or hurricane season, they cannot stop the winds from blowing anymore than they can stop volcanoes from erupting or rivers from overflowing or tsunamis from stretching out the boundaries of the sea.

We need prophets as much as we need scientists. Prophets foretell in ways that scientists cannot, help prepare our hearts, and help us to understand the spiritual forces at work while scientists help us prepare for action and understand the natural forces at work. Let's listen to both.

PACIFIC NW – VANCOUVER B.C & SEATTLE

Prophetic minister Terry Bennett has a track record of

amazing encounters with an angel of the Lord who released various dates regarding geo-political events to come. Among them was the prediction of a 9.1 earthquake in Japan that occurred in 2011.

Terry has actually experienced several visions where the angel Gabriel visited him. During one visitation, Gabriel released the headlines of major news stories that would occur between 2011 and 2015. (See Terry's website for a list of "headline news" http://www.terrybennett.net/)

Among the headline news revealed by Gabriel during a visitation on December 25, 2010 were the following:

"Canadian Quake Shocks British Columbia – Vancouver Affected"
"Sleepless in Seattle – Mt. Rainier Awakens While Residents Lose Sleep"
"The Dark Night of the Soul – Plume Cloud Covers Over Half of the U.S."

One thing the Lord spoke to him about was an impending earthquake that would shatter the Pacific Northwest from Vancouver, British Columbia to Seattle. Terry had no idea of the fault lines in the region including the Cascadia subduction zone and the Whidbey fault lines—either of which could set off an earthquake that would demolish the entire region. One city collapsing is a major disaster, but two cities at once would overwhelm the region. Terry also did not know that in 2011, emergency management planners were already collaborating between the two countries to prepare response and recovery plans for just such a scenario. However, what Terry saw and heard was more than an earthquake. In the vision, he stood in Vancouver and looked south where he saw a volcano erupting. In the same time frame, an earthquake and tsunami occurred as if a triple whammy disaster was unfolding simultaneously.

"Something the Lord told me in 1999, when I was

standing in California praying about the prophetic words given to many about an impending catastrophic earthquake. The Lord rebuked me and said, 'You prophets are always talking about what's going to happen in California but I want you to understand that the greater fault line is in the Pacific NW.' He told me that he would release three things—an earthquake, tsunami and volcano—not just one."

Later, Gabriel visited Terry again and gave him an actual date for the Vancouver to Seattle devastating quake. I will not give the actual date here. Suffice it to say, I heard from reputable intercessors who sense that it could occur as early as September 2011.

Since I live in the Pacific North West and my house is situated on an island located approximately one hour north of Seattle and one hour south of Vancouver, BC, I started researching scientific predictions on an impending quake in the region. What I discovered in August 2011, sent chills down my spine.

Scientists were panicked about a deep tremor occurring three months ahead of schedule. This ETS burst on July 23, 2011 right under the Washington State Capitol building (perhaps spiritually symbolic) and started moving slowly north. Another one started in early August. Scientists believe that a major earthquake event would be triggered by an ETS.

I immediately purchased earthquake insurance and started praying peace into the earth. I stocked up on a week's supply of food, water, and emergency supplies in case I needed to camp out on my property and stashed it in a place easily accessible in case the house totally collapsed. Then, I told neighbors how they could access my cache if they needed it since I was usually out of town. Why not be practical? Even the Proverbs 31 woman could laugh at the days to come—because she was prepared. Prepare for what you can, be at peace, forget-about-it and enjoy life.

Meanwhile, I alerted my friend and fellow islander, filmmaker Michael Lineau (who has produced PBS documentaries on the region's volcanoes, earthquakes and disaster preparation for families and businesses available at http://www.globalnetproductions.com) about the ETS, and Michael immediately sent out a prayer alert email explaining the significance of an ETS to many intercessors:

"In my film Cascadia, I interviewed a Canadian Seismologist about something that he began studying several years ago called ETS -Episodic Tremor and Slip. Every 14-15 months seismologists have detected a roughly M7 earthquake happening in the Cascadia Region, in very slow motion for several weeks as opposed to regular earthquakes where energy is released over seconds or minutes. No one can feel them, but sensitive instruments record them and it has piqued the curiosity of seismologists ever since. They believe that it is during one of these slips that an M9+ Megathrust earthquake and tsunami would most likely be triggered!

This seismology lab (http://www.pnsn.org/WEBICORDER/DEEPTREM/summer2011.html) detected an EARLY ETS! THE NEXT ONE WAS SCHEDULED FOR OCTOBER OR NOVEMBER OF 2011, BUT THEY SAY IN THIS REPORT THAT IT IS HAPPENING NOW. They are scrambling to put instruments in the field to try to record it. It caught them off guard and it is the first time I have seen them use the words "double panicked". I have known these people for 31 years. The seismologist who wrote this article was the one that detected that Mount St. Helens was rumbling to life before anything happened on the surface. Interesting that the tremor "hovered" in Olympia until August 5th. On August 6th we were in Olympia praying with a group of Intercessors."

In addition to that early tremor, a second deep tremor struck the Olympic Peninsula and started moving slowly north during the first week in August. A couple of small earthquakes under 4.0 were felt in the region. As a result, local newspapers started running stories about the scientists' reports and disaster preparedness. An article in the Seattle Times on August 13, 2011 titled, "Free FEMA program models catastrophic disasters" (http://seattletimes.nwsource.com/html/localnews/2015900660_apwaseattledisastermodeling1stldwritethru.html) also brought attention to the potential of a huge earthquake coming sometime soon:

"... Of particular worry to government agencies—and emergency planners like Schelling—is the 680-mile long Cascadia fault line, which runs just 50 miles off Washington's shore. Scientists have found that a big 8.0 to 9.0 earthquake has hit that fault line about every 500 years. The last one struck in 1700.

According to a 2005 study that used Hazus data, such a strong earthquake would level parts of the region, bringing landslides, tsunamis, fires, and spilling hazardous materials among other disastrous effects."

Given the information from scientists and Terry's and other prophets' prophetic insight, a major earthquake in the Seattle to Vancouver, BC region is more likely to occur in September 2012 than in September 2011. If the "predictable" ETS events occur every 14-15 months and the last one felt was in July 2011, the potential for the next major earthquake to occur in September 2012 is great. It is during those ETS events that earthquakes were noted in 2011 and scientists predict that the likelihood of a major earthquake could be set off during a deep tremor event. But what do we really know? The earth could slip and quake tomorrow.

CALIFORNIA EARTHQUAKE PROPHECIES

Many prophets speak about a horribly destructive earthquake demolishing Los Angeles. Here are two prophetic perspectives on what might happen: Rick Joyner and Bob

Jones both talk about an impending earthquake and believe that Californians should ask God if they should move out of the state. To balance the doomsday predictions, Dr. Bill Hamon and Kim Clement reveal the mercy of God who is able to stop it and how we can co-labor with God to transform the region through prayer and blessing.

What are the signs that the Los Angeles earthquake would alter the typography of the state? Bob believes that the tectonic plates are under so much pressure that a volcano will erupt first and the eruption will signal an immanent earthquake along the San Andreas Fault. Prophetic minister Bob Jones, now in his early 80's, has been around Charismatic circles for decades (http://www.bobjones.org/). Considered a "parabolic prophet," Bob often speaks in stories or ties his prophetic words to stories. During a "Blue Moon Conference" hosted by Larry Randolph, Bob stated this:

"I believe the next one is getting ready to happen when this volcano erupts when the plates can't take the pressure anymore. And I believe the pressure is melting the plates down there to where this has got to be vented, and these earthquakes are just a sign of what is getting ready to happen. It's getting ready to blow! When it does, it will break loose all the way to the Sea of Cortez, right up the Los Angeles River. And that plate in there will separate from the United States, and you can drive a boat up that river. You can go from the Gulf of Cortez to the Pacific Ocean. And Death Valley will be a great inland sea. And we aren't far from that."

Dr. Bill Hamon, founder of Christian International Ministries, believes the opposite. In an article posted on his website titled, "Dr. Bill Hamon's Prophetic Word for California Concerning Impending Earthquake" (http://www.christianinternational.com/index.php?option=com_zoo&task=item&item_id=2711&Itemid=33), he writes that forces may be set in motion but our prayer is more powerful.

"There is a divine principle that God established when he made man upon the earth and gave him dominion over all things concerning earth. "God will do nothing upon the earth without man's participation." Adam and Eve lost that full authority by their disobedience to God. Jesus came to earth and became God manifest in a human body. Jesus, by obedience even to death on the cross and resurrection from the dead, restored to all mankind in Christ original participation with authority and dominion. That is why the Church can be the determining factor for what happens or doesn't happen on the earth.

The Science Daily News stated in their paper on April 16, 2008: "California has more than a 99% chance of having a magnitude 6.7 or larger earthquake within the next 30 years. The likelihood of a major quake of magnitude 7.5 or greater in the next 30 years is 46%, and such a quake is most likely to occur in the southern half of the state." Only the prayers of the Saints can prevent it from happening.

...God wants Christians to be more kingdom-of-God conscious than earthquake conscious. Pray with faith and reality for God's kingdom to come and His will to be done in California as it is in heaven. God wants to send a manifestation of His glory beyond anything the earth has ever seen. God's declared ultimate purpose is for the earth to be filled with the glory of the Lord as the waters cover the sea (Numbers 14:21; Habakuk 2:14). The Church needs to pray, preach, and demonstrate the kingdom in faith more than being fearful of earthquakes.

My prophetic admonition to California Christians is for them to take no action based on fear, but only move by divine revelation and faith. Jesus is our only protection and provision regardless of where we are in America or anywhere in the world. I pray for the spirit of wisdom and revelation to rest upon all Christians in California. Amen."

During a conference held in Anaheim, California on June 25, 2005, (http://kimclementvault.com/prophecyread. asp?num=183&keyword=california) prophetic minister Kim

Clement predicted a more symbolic earthquake and tsunami. Originally from South Africa, Kim moved his ministry to California a year ago and ministers in a style that the Hollywood set can appreciate—often playing a prophetic piano rift while prophesying. He said:

"I want to visit California, and then I want to rest my feet. I wanted to judge the unrighteous and then rest my case, but I heard somebody praying. I heard somebody praying and I stopped. A great tsunami that you don't even know about, says the Spirit. Oh, the desire of the religious to drop this piece of land called California into the sea. But, as I stood before Abraham and he said, 'Lord for the sake of just ten', and I found that there were more than ten in California. And I will let you live to see a spiritual tsunami in this state called California. California, you shall live!"

While Kim prophesied that a major earthquake would not disrupt California to the extent that other prophets like Bob Jones and Rick Joyner have prophesied for years, he went on to predict a volcanic eruption—again symbolic but also likely in the natural. He prophesied on March 25, 2011 from Nashville, Tennessee (http://kimclementvault.com/prophecyread.asp?num=453&keyword=mountains):

"'Watch the mountains,' says the Lord, 'Watch the mountains as they begin to erupt. You see, the earth is busy—from deep within; it has erupted from within. Now it's going to go to the mountains,' says the Lord. 'There will be minimal loss of lives, but the earth erupting represents an eruption of the Spirit of the Living God upon the nations of the earth!'

The Lord says, 'Watch the mountains! They will erupt and smoke shall come from them, and the people will say, "Oh my God, it is the end!"' But God said, 'It is the beginning, it is the beginning of labor pains, for something is about to be born. An eruption of My Spirit as never before, and I shall bring forth something that will reach every nation on the earth,' says the Lord.'"

THE CONSEQUENCES OF DIVIDING JERUSALEM

In addition to predicting the California earthquake, Bob Jones believed one would strike Washington DC in the near future (one did hit Washington DC in the summer of 2011). However, the potential for larger impact beyond the Capitol and tied to the Capitol may be completely preventable. Bob predicts that the New Madrid fault line in the mid-west will shift dramatically in the future if the U.S. Government shifts its alliance with Israel.

During a conference called "Eyes & Ears" hosted by Jeff Jansen in May 2011, Bob said:

"If NATO troops are used to divide Jerusalem, and the U.S. is a large part of NATO troops, it will be the last thing we do as a nation. The New Madrid Fault Line will divide if we divide Jerusalem. We need to pray for Jerusalem continually. There are plans to invade Israel and divide it. The Church can stop these plans. The church should be praying for Israel continually. You don't really want to know what will happen if we divide Jerusalem. The Mississippi River will cut 35 miles wide. Five of our greatest cities will be gone. This is a warning. Our nuclear plants will melt down there. And this nation will become a third-rate power, a bankrupt nation. If this happens, we will be debt-slaves to other nations and our food supplies will be sent to other nations.

Jerusalem is His footstool. If you check history, every time we've touched anything dealing with Israel, we get hit immediately. Hurricane Katrina was no accident. We gave Gaza away and we got Katrina. You check back every time there is a financial collapse, we had butted into Israel's business. That arrogance and that pride, if we seek to divide Jerusalem in half, everything along the Mississippi River will be gone. The great lakes will break through to the Mississippi and run down to the Gulf.

Keep your hands off of Israel."

In late September, 2011, the issue of recognizing a Palestinian State came before the United Nations, calling for Israel to give up more land and divide Jerusalem. The issue will never go away given the anti-Semitism and anti-Israeli sentiment growing around the world, fueled by radical extremists. The consequences of such a vote in favor of creating a Palestinian State, a people-group that refuses to "recognize" Israel and plans for Israel's total destruction, are sure to be catastrophic if Israel is pressured to comply. According to Bob, if you touch the apple of God's eye, God won't be happy and spiritual forces will be unleashed in the earth—as it is on heaven. God blesses those who bless Israel. Perhaps 2012 or beyond will see a major earthquake rip our nation in half. Our political and personal agendas do ripple through the atmosphere, impacting others for generations to come.

MORE SHAKE AND QUAKE COMING

Prophetic minister Larry Randolph (www.larryrandolph.com) lives outside of Nashville, Tennessee. He also speaks about impending earthquakes—in places not normally seen. But he is also a believer in the power and authority of the believer to calm the earth and increase damage control. In 2011, Larry said during a conference held in Tennessee called "Blue Moon":

"This summer the Lord talked to me about seven earthquakes coming, each on up to 7.0 and 8.0 on the Richter scale. Within a few months, we had three or four of those. There are two or three more of those coming. There are some great shakings to come next year and we are going to see them in some very extreme places where we didn't think they would happen. So God is arising to shake terribly the earth, so we need to pray against some of those destructions and that they will be reduced."

THE WOES OF 2012 & FUTURE DROUGHTS & FAMINES

On several occasions, prophetic minister John Paul Jackson has prophesied about food and water shortages, civil unrest on a massive scale impacting cities, increasing unemployment, and political and economic depression. During an interview with Sid Roth (http://www.sidroth.org/site/New s2?page=NewsArticle&id=8629&news_iv_ctrl=0&abbr=tv), he revealed that some of John Paul's predictions have come true. One ominous and vague reference echoes in my mind clearly from time to time. After an angelic visitation where many future events were revealed to John Paul, he said this, "I kept hearing an angel saying in a deep loud voice, 'The woes of 2012. The woes of 2012. The woes of 2012.' I don't know what those woes are. The angel did not tell me about those woes." However, the angel told him plenty about woes beyond 2012.

One of the things he saw was a coming drought when water would become a huge issue. He believes that, at some point in the future, city tap water will be more expensive than oil.

"We're talking about water that's normally fairly inexpensive becoming very expensive. In fact, various cities in the United States would have to evacuate thousands of people because there wouldn't be enough water in the reservoirs and in the aquifers that they get the water from, to get water to all the people."

Along with the water shortage would be a food shortage—but not necessarily tied into drought conditions.

"I saw a blight coming to hybrid seeds, and that would bring a type of famine to the United States. So the hybrid seeds that have been propagated by various corporations, supposedly resistant to all kinds of things, will actually allow for a blight to come. Some of the seeds won't break the ground. Some of the seeds will break the ground but never bear fruit, and so you'll end up seeing green out in the fields. There will be enough rain for them in certain areas, but they won't come to seed. So there won't be the corn that would normally be in the ear. There won't be the wheat that is normally in the head of wheat. So that creates a major food shortage."

SOLAR DISTURBANCES & POLAR SHIFTS

Terry Bennett and other prophets also saw solar disturbances coming, beginning in 2012, that would seemed apocalyptic and dramatic, frightening in their impact on earth. According to Terry's word given during a conference in Kansas City in spring of 2011, solar disturbances would alter life as we know it.

He believes that the sun's rising and setting was altered throughout the earth as the earth tilted and time zones changed. Weather patterns became unpredictable and hurricane seasons were so altered that hurricanes started coming at times totally out of season. The gravitational pull surrounding the earth increased and satellites were yanked right out of the sky.

"Actually, the sun caused other planets within our solar system to act up. They aligned, I don't know how to explain this, I am not a scientist, but they aligned in a funny pattern. It was not a straight line. They aligned themselves in a funny pattern and when they did that, they also affected the earth. But in comparison it was 95% solar as the sun did what it did and brought rolling blackouts, electrical disruption, water distribution disruption because it is run by machinery. It was major throughout the earth."

"I saw then, the sun did this weird, funny thing. I do not even know how to describe it but its effect on the earth was incredible. It was like a storm with flares and all of that and the gravitational pull of the earth increased. The magnetism of the earth increased. The tilt of the earth was altered so that time itself changed all over the earth. The satellites were both blinded and some of them were yanked out right out of the sky. He blinded the communications of the earth. Cell phones, all types of things, military hardware, commercial hardware, people were blinded, GPS was useless, the magnetic north itself altered which affected all forms of travel especially by sea and by land. They used to be guided by the North Star but the North Star will not be in the same position so it altered...

[a polar shift]. It was dramatic.

Everything that deals with waves, sound waves and that type of thing was dramatically affected. Types of equipment, such as pace makers, were disrupted. A lot of machinery in hospitals was not reliable or it was useless to them. I could see that in airports, in military installations."

SCIENTISTS COMMENT ON POLAR SHIFTS AND SOLAR STORMS

Taking a look at the science behind solar storms and polar shifts predicted by those who interpret psychics and mysterious historical calendars can help us put celestial matters in perspective. NASA's website actually devoted a FAQ page to handle all the questions surrounding 2012 and the "impending doom" from outer space predicted by New Age writers. While NASA representatives comment on asteroids, they do not mention here that an asteroid is indeed scheduled to hit earth—but not until the year 2182. According to scientists, with an estimated probability of 0.07%, Apollo asteroid 1999 RQ36 could hit the Earth.

Official NASA comments about the coming years should bring peace to those who feel unsettled. However, scientists did not create the world, they only seek to understand it. Only one Being created the world. And His ways are unfathomable.

What follows is the article from the NASA website that seeks to address New Age psychic predictions and still the fears so many are stirring up in our society.

"2012: BEGINNING OF THE END OR WHY THE WORLD WON'T END?"

(http://www.nasa.gov/topics/earth/features/2012.html)

> *"There apparently is a great deal of interest in celestial bodies, and their locations and trajectories at the end of the calendar year 2012. Now, I for one love a good book or movie as much as the next guy. But the stuff flying around through cyberspace, TV and the movies is not based on science. There is even a fake NASA news release out there..."*
> - Don Yeomans, NASA senior research scientist

Remember the Y2K scare? It came and went without much of a whimper because of adequate planning and analysis of the situation. Impressive movie special effects aside, Dec. 21, 2012, won't be the end of the world as we know. It will, however, be another winter solstice.

Much like Y2K, 2012 has been analyzed and the science of the end of the Earth thoroughly studied. Contrary to some of the common beliefs out there, the science behind the end of the world quickly unravels when pinned down to the 2012 timeline. Below, NASA scientists answer several questions that we're frequently asked regarding 2012.

Q: Are there any threats to the Earth in 2012? Many Internet websites say the world will end in December 2012.

A: Nothing bad will happen to the Earth in 2012. Our planet has been getting along just fine for more than 4 billion years, and credible scientists worldwide know of no threat associated with 2012.

Q: What is the origin of the prediction that the world will end in 2012?

A: The story started with claims that Nibiru, a supposed planet discovered by the Sumerians, is headed toward Earth. This catastrophe was initially predicted for May 2003, but when nothing happened the doomsday date was moved forward to December 2012. Then these two fables were linked to the end of one of the cycles in the ancient Mayan calendar at the winter solstice in 2012—hence the predicted doomsday date of December 21, 2012.

Q: Does the Mayan calendar end in December 2012?

A: Just as the calendar you have on your kitchen wall does not cease to exist after December 31, the Mayan calendar does not cease to exist on December 21, 2012. This date is the end of the Mayan long-count period but then—just as your calendar begins again on January 1—another long-count period begins for the Mayan calendar.

Q: Could phenomena occur where planets align in a way that impacts Earth?

A: There are no planetary alignments in the next few decades. Earth will not cross the galactic plane in 2012, and even if these alignments were to occur, their effects on the Earth would be negligible. Each December the Earth and sun align with the approximate center of the Milky Way Galaxy but that is an annual event of no consequence.

Q: Is there a planet or brown dwarf called Nibiru or Planet X or Eris that is approaching the Earth and threatening our planet with widespread destruction?

A: Nibiru and other stories about wayward planets are an Internet hoax. There is no factual basis for these claims. If Nibiru or Planet X were real and headed for an encounter with the Earth in 2012, astronomers would have been tracking it for at least the past decade, and it would be visible by now to the naked eye. Obviously, it does not exist. Eris is real, but it is a dwarf planet similar to Pluto that will remain in the outer solar system; the closest it can come to Earth is about 4 billion miles.

Q: What is the polar shift theory? Is it true that the earth's crust does a 180-degree rotation around the core in a matter of days if not hours?

A: A reversal in the rotation of Earth is impossible. There are slow movements of the continents (for example Antarctica was near the equator hundreds of millions of years ago), but that is irrelevant to claims of reversal of the rotational poles. However, many of the disaster websites pull a bait-and-shift to fool people. They claim a relationship between the rotation and the magnetic polarity of Earth, which does change irregularly, with a magnetic reversal taking place every 400,000 years on average. As far as we know, such a magnetic reversal doesn't cause any harm to life on Earth. A magnetic reversal is very unlikely to happen in the next few millennia, anyway.

Q: Is the Earth in danger of being hit by a meteor in 2012?

A: The Earth has always been subject to impacts by comets and asteroids, although big hits are very rare. The last big impact was 65 million years ago, and that led to the extinction of the dinosaurs. Today NASA astronomers are carrying out a survey called the Spaceguard Survey to find any large near-Earth asteroids long before they hit. We have already determined that there are no threatening asteroids as large as the one that killed the dinosaurs. All this work is done openly with the discoveries posted every day on the NASA NEO Program Office website, so you can see for yourself that nothing is predicted to hit in 2012.

Q: How do NASA scientists feel about claims of pending doomsday?

A: For any claims of disaster or dramatic changes in 2012, where is the science? Where is the evidence? There is none, and for all the fictional assertions, whether they are made in books, movies, documentaries or over the Internet, we cannot change that simple fact. There is no credible evidence for any of the assertions made in support of unusual events taking place in December 2012.

Q: Is there a danger from giant solar storms predicted for 2012?

A: Solar activity has a regular cycle, with peaks approximately every 11 years. Near these activity peaks, solar flares can cause some interruption of satellite communications, although engineers are learning how to build electronics that are protected against most solar storms. But there is no special risk associated with 2012. The next solar maximum will occur in the 2012-2014 time frame and is predicted to be an average solar cycle, no different than previous cycles throughout history.

SO WHAT DO WE DO?

Science and prophecy sometimes merge and sometimes diverge. No one really knows exactly how the galaxy works and interacts with the earth and its atmosphere, or how the earth responds to natural and spiritual events. Mystics and scientists disagree often about events to come. Scientists can confirm events and mystics often interpret events according to their spiritual understanding and imagination—in the aftermath. However, prophets have often been right in their predictions, as scientists have been in theirs. No matter what you choose to believe, there is one who knows the beginning from the end—the Creator. And He is worth knowing. You access Him by faith, simply by asking God to reveal Himself to you, to open the eyes of your understanding to know Jesus. God will lead you to Himself and into the truth...if you really want to seek the Truth. Those who seek Him will find Him.

It doesn't take a prophetic word to know that the earth is alive and vibrant and natural disasters will happen. Find the purpose of God in your life and seek Him for how you are to respond. Perhaps you are called to help. Perhaps you are called to pray. All of us are clearly being called to prepare spiritually and mentally for the days to come. How big is Christ in you? Is He the hope of glory to you—and can He be so big in you that you will have the mental and spiritual wherewithal to release His glory to others in a day of need? We Christians should be able to rise and shine during a needed and darkened time.

Be the light of the world today...at least in your own neighborhood.

Julia Loren is the author of several books including: *Shifting Shadows of Supernatural Power, Shifting Shadows of Supernatural Experiences, Supernatural Anointing, When God Says Yes, & Divine Intervention: True Stories of Heaven Invading Earth.*
www.divineinterventionbooks.com

THE DAY THE WORLD CHANGED

By Rick Joyner

There are demarcation points in history where a turn is made and the world starts down a different path. March 11, 2011 will be remembered as one of those days. The 9.0 earthquake that rocked Japan, moving the entire island an estimated 8 feet, actually shifted the earth on its axis enough to change the length of our days and nights. It may not have been enough to notice, but even a slight change on our axis can have major consequences over time. The same is true with the social and economic consequence this earthquake, tsunami, and nuclear meltdown will have on modern civilization.

It was twenty-two years ago that I first heard Bob Jones talk about a major earthquake that would be coming to Japan. He said that it would set off cataclysmic events. Thousands have heard Bob predict quakes and other natural events with astonishing accuracy. One of the most dramatic was the last San Francisco quake. He foresaw that the quake would be centered in Northern California but south of San Francisco. He said that it would be 7.0 on the Richter Scale, that the bridges would be dangerous, and that "the world will witness it." Bob shared this at conferences and churches for months before it hit that fall. It struck during the first game of the World Series that year, which was being played in San Francisco, and it was being broadcast to 160 nations who witnessed it live, accurately fulfilling all that Bob had predicted, including how the world would see it.

Many prophetic people were shown the next quake that hit Southern California, and they were told that this was a warning of another much greater one to come. We shared this in many churches and conferences in Southern California. When it struck, we were astonished at how even the churches responded, downplaying its message, and some even boasting that Californians could handle anything. We felt that the quake we had clearly predicted, with many details that were accurate, had virtually no impact on the people, even some of the strongest Christians who had heard the warnings.

When one of the most well-known Christian leaders in the area asked me what could be done to delay or lesson this quake, I was given "a word of wisdom" that the only commandment with a promise was to honor our fathers and mothers, and the promise was that "it may be well with you, and that you may live long on the earth" (see Ephesians 6:3). The Lord showed me that one way we could do this was the way Israel did it, which was to drink from the wells that our fathers have dug. Spiritually, this meant to partake of their teachings. When I preached this in Pasadena, Lou Engle picked it up, wrote a book about it, and has in a most remarkable way carried this message to the nation through The Call.

Has it worked? I think Lou's work and that of many others have given us the time that we've had. While many were still receiving revelation about the coming big one, and many were expecting it, Bob Jones was adamant that it would not come until the major one hit Japan that he had seen. When the major quake hit Kobe, Japan, Bob was sure that was not the one he had seen. When Bob walked into the service last Sunday after the recent 9.0 quake, tsunami, and nuclear meltdown, I immediately asked him if this was the one. I've never seen such concern in Bob's face as he answered, "You know what this means."

WHAT DOES IT MEAN?

It marks a demarcation point after which great change

will come to the whole world, including an ultimate meltdown of the economy. It will also be followed by a major quake on the West Coast of the United States.

Of course, when and where on the west coast that this major quake is going to hit are important questions. Bob was not given a timing on this quake but was only told that it would not come before the big one he had been shown in Japan. Now it can come. However, this does not necessarily mean that it is immediate. It could come today, or it could still be years away. We are praying that it still will be delayed so that everyone who will hear the warning, and should move, will be able to do this in an orderly way.

This does not mean that everyone there, even those who may be near ground zero, should move. Some may be called by God to stay and be used during this impending catastrophe. However, until now, we have counseled all who asked if they should leave the West Coast not to do this unless they heard from the Lord to do so. Now we will begin counseling everyone to leave unless they hear from the Lord to stay.

Until now, I have prayed for leaders who would have the understanding, wisdom, and courage to make the changes needed to avoid this economic meltdown. Now I am praying for leaders with the understanding, wisdom, and courage to lead us through what is now inevitable.

THE NATURE OF PROPHECY

As we are told in I Corinthians 13, we see in part, know in part, and prophesy in part. No one has the whole picture, so to get the whole picture, we need to put the parts together. This is why in the Scriptures that say such things as in Amos 3:7, "Surely the Lord GOD does nothing unless He reveals His secret counsel to His servants the prophets," it is always plural, not just a single prophet. No one prophet, or prophetic movement, has the whole revelation. That is a major reason why we need each other.

We know many prophetically gifted people who have seen different aspects of this major quake coming. I do not know anyone at this writing who has what I consider to be a trustworthy timing on it. We will seek to compile these prophecies and share anything we feel is important in future Special Bulletins. As we are told in Proverbs 4:18, "the path of the righteous is like the light of dawn, that shines brighter and brighter until the full day." It is as we walk and as we need it that the Lord tends to give us more insight. I am just sharing what we do have now.

WHAT WILL THE ECONOMIC MELTDOWN LOOK LIKE?

It can mean many things, but one thing it does not mean is the end of the world, and it does not have to be the end of America as a free Republic. We can emerge from this stronger and better than ever, even economically stronger and better. However, we are entering some of the most dangerous times we have ever had to navigate. Without the right leadership and the right resolve of the nation, which will only come by the grace of God, we can also fall to a terrible tyranny.

Two aspects of this meltdown that I have confidence in is the dollar losing its value with bartering being the currency for a period of time, and that there will be a time when banks are closed and what we have deposited in them will not be available. Obviously, if the dollar has lost its value, we would not even bother to get out what we have deposited in the banks, so it does not seem that these will come at the same time. It could also be that things of value we have deposited in safety deposit boxes will not be reachable.

A DEADLY DELUSION

In II Timothy 4:3-4, we are given a most sobering warning:

> For the time will come when they will not endure sound doctrine; but wanting to have their ears tickled, they will accumulate for themselves teachers in accordance to their own desires; and will turn away their ears from the truth and will turn aside to myths.

One of the greatest weaknesses of American Christians is the way that so many have been conditioned against hearing anything they perceive to be negative. They have become the fulfillment of the biblical prophecy above. Many of these have already paid a terrible price for their delusion, and we do have a sure hope that through anything which comes, we can have unshakable peace and joy in the Lord. Even so, very difficult times are coming upon us in which the wise can be prepared and can prevail. These can actually be the most prosperous times for those who are the wisest. The wise win souls, which is why the next verse in II Timothy states: "But you, be sober in all things, endure hardship, do the work of an evangelist, fulfill your ministry."

This is going to be the greatest time of harvest of all time. Our preparation needs to be far more devoted to the spiritual than the natural. We can't just hoard for ourselves, but we must think about how we can be the salt and light we are called to be in anything that happens.

Change has to come. Many of the basic underpinnings of a strong and lasting economy that our nation was founded upon have been abandoned. This has kept us on the edge of the cliff in a most dangerous place for a long time. There has been no strength or resolve in our leadership to make the difficult but necessary decisions to begin moving us away from the cliff. Before the quake hit, fear had begun rising that the Japanese economy, which had been on the edge for nearly two decades, simply could not hold out much longer and would very soon slide off the cliff. This would cause the others who were tottering to go down too. Again, this crisis was impending even before the earthquake, tsunami, and nuclear meltdown.

Based on the sure evidence of Scripture, in everything that we see like this, we believe that with prayer and repentance these things can be avoided. One example of this was how Nineveh was spared after Jonah had prophesied their doom. For years, we have been praying that there would be the kind of awakening and repentance that would enable us to avoid this whole scenario. However, we also knew that when the quake hit in Japan, these were no longer going to be avoided. Therefore, our strategy has changed from trying to wake up the church so that it would not have to happen, to trying to get God's people ready for it. We can still pray for the Lord's mercy and grace through them. The Lord does prefer mercy over judgment, but there is a time when judgment is inevitable, and we have now crossed that Rubicon.

JUDGMENT IS MERCY

A number of different judgments of God are in Scripture—only one is condemnation and only one is destruction. The rest are discipline from the Lord for those He loves. We should be far more afraid if we go without His discipline. The discipline that is about to come to our nation is because He loves us. We are told in I Corinthians 11:31 that if we would judge ourselves, He would not have to judge us. That would be even better, and He has given us much time to do this, but now He is going to have to help us.

THE RIGHT PATH

As we have already quoted from Proverbs 4:18, if we are on the right path, our lives should be getting brighter and brighter. This does not mean that we will not have trials, but that we should be able to see them with increasing clarity, and we should be able to see where our feet should go with increasing light. This is true for those who are on the path of the righteous regardless of the circumstances. If this is not what is happening in your life, you have missed a turn somewhere. In the Lord, the wrong road never turns into the right road. If we have missed a turn, the only thing we can do is to return to where we missed the turn and get back on the right road. That is called "repentance."

Through everything that is coming we must live by faith and not be controlled by fear. Unstable and immature people will receive just about any warning with fear and that cannot be helped. Some believe their presumption is faith, and that because they believe it, nothing bad will happen. We cannot let such people control us either.

America and many other nations have drifted from sound doctrine. This includes sound economic policy in ways that cannot be sustained. It would have been much easier to correct these bad practices before a collapse, and we will now have to do it in the midst of much greater challenges. However, it can still be done. America has a destiny that we have not yet fulfilled. God has not given up on us, but we could go no further in the direction we have been going.

The inevitable economic unraveling may not happen all at once. It may not become manifest immediately that it is happening. In recent times, our leaders have become very good at disguising the true condition we're in. They may be doing this with good intentions, just not wanting to cause panic to those who could not do anything about the situation anyway, while they find a way out. They may be disguising the truth because they do not understand it themselves. Either way, what is happening in the world economy seems to be a striking parallel to the way the Japanese government has been trying to deal with the nuclear crisis—they're telling us one thing but the instruments are telling us something else. They seem to get one fire under control and another worse one breaks out—the meltdown continues and we keep finding out that things are really much worse than they've been telling us.

Again, as a pastor and as a watchman, my strategy has now changed from praying and seeking to intercede with our leaders to make the necessary changes, to helping God's people prepare to go through the collapse that is now inevitable. How do we prepare?

THE OPPORTUNITY OF CRISIS

It is noteworthy that the same Chinese word for "crisis" is the same word for opportunity. This may truly be the greatest opportunity we have ever had. As we see in Daniel 2, when the statue that represents the kingdoms of this world begins to collapse, then the little rock that struck at the feet of this statue will begin to grow into a mountain, which in Scripture often represents government. Then that rock keeps on growing until it fills the entire earth. The kingdom of God that the Lord has had His people praying for these last two thousand years is also inevitable. It is surely coming, and we can live in it now.

As the governments of this world collapse, God's government will become more manifest. As the economies of this world collapse, God's economy will become more manifest. The kingdom will not fully come until the King returns, but a job that He left for His people to do before He returned was to preach the gospel, or good news, of His coming kingdom. We do have good news to share, not bad.

In Isaiah 40, we are called to help prepare the way for His kingdom by building a highway. This highway is the road on which His kingdom will come. This highway will bring the other mountains and hills down, and it will raise up the valleys and low places. The entire chapter gives a good panorama of what is happening in the nations right now.

When Israel was taken into exile into Babylon, the Lord gave a remarkable counsel to His people through Jeremiah:

> *Thus says the LORD of hosts, the God of Israel, to all the exiles whom I have sent into exile from Jerusalem to Babylon,*
>
> *'Build houses and live in them; and plant gardens, and eat their produce.*
>
> *Take wives and become the fathers of sons and daughters, and take wives for your sons and give your daughters to husbands, that they may bear sons and daughters; and multiply there and do not decrease.*
>
> *'Seek the welfare of the city where I have sent you into exile, and pray to the LORD on its behalf; for in its welfare you will have welfare.' (Jeremiah 29:4-7)*

In a sense, Christians, who are citizens of another kingdom, have likewise been in exile waiting for their redemption and the kingdom of God to come. It is the right thing to do to seek the welfare of whatever nation we have been called to live in, and to put down roots there as Israel was counseled above. However, God's people are also to be a distinct and separate people in many ways and were not to defile themselves with the immorality, perversions, and idolatry of Babylon. Those in exile were to maintain their devotion to the laws that God had given them to make them a distinct people for His purposes. The same is true of Christians. Being a part of our nation and seeking its good, while building our own homes and families, does not mean that we compromise the basic teachings of the kingdom.

Those who have lived by kingdom economic principles have built on a kingdom that cannot be shaken, and they will not be shaken when everything else is. If we have not obeyed the Lord in this, and have foolishly built our estates by the principles of the world instead of the principles of the kingdom, there is still hope. We can repent, be forgiven, and be restored to a right foundation. This does not mean that we will not suffer or will not lose what was built on a wrong foundation, but we still can recover and build on a right foundation. We can do this personally and nationally.

What will the economic meltdown look like? Hebrews 12:25-29 states it quite clearly:

> *See to it that you do not refuse Him who is speaking. For if those did not escape when they refused him who warned them on earth, much less shall we escape who turn away from Him who warns from heaven.*

> *And His voice shook the earth then, but now He has promised, saying, "YET ONCE MORE I WILL SHAKE NOT ONLY THE EARTH, BUT ALSO THE HEAVEN."*

> *And this expression, "Yet once more," denotes the removing of those things which can be shaken, as of created things, in order that those things which cannot be shaken may remain.*

> *Therefore, since we receive a kingdom that cannot be shaken, let us show gratitude, by which we may offer to God an acceptable service with reverence and awe; for our God is a consuming fire.*

The coming economic meltdown will be the removal of everything that is not built on the kingdom principles that cannot be shaken. Many of the founding principles of our nation and our free market system were kingdom principles. We must return to those as a nation, and we must return to them personally.

We are told in Psalm 89:14 and other places that "righteousness and justice are the foundation of His throne." Righteousness is doing what is right in the sight of the Lord. God's justice requires fair and equitable treatment of all people, judging issues by one standard for all, regardless of their station in life. It was the American devotion to these basic truths that enabled the greatest economic engine in history to be built here. It has been a departure from these basic principles that has caused every major problem we're now facing as a nation. We must have a national repentance.

In the Lord's teaching about those who build their houses on the rock rather than on sand, we are told several things that are crucial for the times we're now in. First, the storms beat against both houses, but only the house built on the rock would stand. The storms are coming, but if we have built well we will stand.

To build on the rock, we must hear the words of the Lord, and then we have to obey them. As we are told in other places, hearing His words and not obeying them is to bring an even more severe judgment. I have been a Christian for forty years now, and from the time I was converted, I remember hearing warnings about the times that we're now in. The Lord has spoken loudly, clearly, and abundantly. Many heard, but it does not seem that as many have obeyed.

In many ways, I have been guilty of this too, and I have paid the price for it. Even so, in every case where I have seen it, humbled myself and repented, not trying to cover up or make excuses, His grace has been abundant. I went through a bankruptcy and lost virtually everything I had spent years and great effort building, and two years later, I came out in an even better place.

His grace is still available for us personally and nationally. We will suffer loss if we have done this, and we can expect to go through some hard times. However, if we repent, turning away from our sins, resolving to live in obedience to Him, we can expect to emerge in a much better place. As we are assured in Romans 14:17, "The kingdom of God is not eating and drinking, but righteousness and peace and joy in the Holy Spirit." It will come in this order too. When we do what is righteous, it will be followed by true peace, which will be followed by true joy.

How long has it been since you've known true peace? How about true joy? These are in your future. Now is the time to set our hearts and minds to obey the Lord and to repent of and correct every way that is not in obedience to Him. If we are going to live in His kingdom, building our lives on that which cannot be shaken and can withstand any storm that comes upon this earth, then we must begin by resolving to live by the key to the kingdom, which we are given in Matthew 6:33-34:

> *But seek first His kingdom and His righteousness; and all these things will be added to you.*
>
> *So do not worry about tomorrow; for tomorrow will care for itself. Each day has enough trouble of its own.*

Christians who are now living, working, or even going to church in the wrong places are there because they made major decisions based on what they wanted or what others wanted them to do, rather than seeking first what the Lord wanted them to do for the sake of His kingdom. To seek His kingdom first, means much more than firing up a prayer here and there for Him to guide us, and then go and immediately do what we want to do. It requires seeking Him until we find Him. When it takes longer than we think it should take to find Him, it could be because we have drifted so far from Him.

Now is the time to do whatever it takes to get in the will of the Lord. There will be an increasingly high price to pay for those who are not. There will be increasing peace and joy for those who are.

Rick Joyner is a prophetic minister and founder of Morningstar Ministries.This article was used with permission and reprinted from his website: http://www.morningstarministries.org/Articles/1000102270/

A DECADE OF REALIGNMENT

by Martin Scott

There is no question that the world is changing and changing fast. The clock helps us understand 'chronos' time, but this decade does not seem to want to keep in step with the clock. It's a decade of rapid change, a time for kingdom advances. At the beginning of the decade I had a dream, the latter part of which was simple yet profound. I watched a 20 and a 10 come down from the sky, the numbers fell on to a see-saw, with the 20 on one side and the 10 on the other. Instantly the 20 outweighed the 10 and the see-saw was unbalanced. Then came an 11 that replaced the 10. It dropped on the see-saw and there was a major swing, but back it went as the 20 still outweighed the 11. This pattern continued for each digit: 12,13, etc. right up to a situation where a 20 came and there was a 20 sitting on both sides. Then as it settled the see-saw was balanced.

We are in a decade of great swings, with a constant attempt to pull things back to the status quo, but by the end of the decade there will be major re-alignments. Our world will look different. Why the realignment? I consider this is due to the Living God who answers prayer. Why the swings back to the status quo? Probably due to two factors: a human (and a church) desire for the familiar and also the work of the enemy to confuse, intimidate and cause fear to rise. It is paramount that we guard our hearts against fear, 'Let not you hearts be troubled' is a word for this time. We must also resist the temptation to run to the familiar for cover. Uncharted territory lies ahead yet in that uncharted terrain is the invitation to enter into the level of first century God-experience expressed in a twenty-first century context. Our participation with God will allow us to live through some of the most wonderful shifts that can be recorded in history.

For some time I have had a quote from Rudolph Bahro, on my screen, that I have often read:

> *"When the forms of an old culture are dying, the new culture is created by a few people who are not afraid to be insecure."*

Culture is always changing, but there are certain times in history when there is a major shift in culture. This is such a time. At a national level we have to see this cultural change take place. Legislation is vital, but the real battle is a cultural one. Laws will be broken, but culture is what shapes a people. Culture acts like an unwritten boundary. Compassionate and just culture that is shaped through godliness is what our lands cry out for. It is also vital that we become committed to impact culture globally. I am very skeptical about most of what is written of 'the Antichrist' and such things, but am very aware that into vacuums will come something / someone to fill the space. The ultimate outcome of the triumph of the kingdom is certain, the immediate generational outworking is in the balance. Change always occurs, but does not always occur at the same rate, and again we are alive at a time when the pace of change, and therefore the opportunity to affect that change is in our hands.

The days of church as a ghetto are ending. The days of embracing / loving our communities and from within, and as part of, those communities, releasing change are here. For the world to change the church has to change, and the church cannot change without two wonderful dynamics coming together. The presence of heaven and the love for the world. The former has been increasing, now the fear barrier has to be broken so that the latter can increase.

THE SHAKING OF ALL THINGS

Knowing the ways of God will help us interpret what we experience. God answers prayer but the answer to prayer is not a straight line. When we pray for our faith to rise the most likely result is that we face trials. In other words there is a process toward the answer that is released when we pray. Hence a new order being established in the Spirit will come through what has been established being shaken (Heb. 12:28) or (in the language of the dream) through the swings of a see-saw.

There are always fresh outpourings of the Spirit but we have lived through a century when the body of Christ has experienced the effects of three global waves of Pentecost. We have also lived through signs such as the Berlin wall coming down, and the tragedy of the twin towers, as well as traumatic tsunamis and earthquakes, and weather patterns that seem out of control. All this speaks loudly; surely creation is crying out. The cry is always one for liberation from bondage and into the purposes of God.

Shifts seem to have two 'sides' to them. The positive and what can seem like the negative. We receive a kingdom that cannot be shaken (positive) through everything being shaken (the process that can appear negative). Realignment means everything will be shaken.

What we have been praying into will help us understand what is taking place. There has been a cry for the power of God, and we are very grateful for the increase in the miraculous. There is more to be experienced, but the calling out to heaven has begun to have a bigger effect than we anticipated. There is healing for bodies and there is also healing for nations that comes through the cross.

Let me begin with a big one. The shaking of imperial power so that true power can be manifested. In the fifteenth year of the reign of Tiberius Caesar... during the high priesthood of Annas and Caiaphas, the word of God came to John son of Zechariah in the desert (Luke 3:1,2).

Luke, the historian is interested in more than dates and personalities. He is interested in recording the impact the presence of the kingdom of God is going to make into the world that was dominated by the Caesars of Rome. He, like his fellow-followers of Jesus, knew that Caesar, despite the claims from Rome, was not 'lord'. A process began in the desert with John, it comes to decisive fulfillment in Jesus as he breaks religious, economic and political power in Jerusalem, in order to pour out the Spirit on his people for testimony in the world. As we read Luke's follow up book we realize that he leaves the narrative unfinished. He leaves us with Paul under house arrest in Rome, proclaiming the kingdom of God. The world where Caesar claimed he was lord was the very same world where Paul made his declarations that Jesus was Lord. There is no mistaking the deep parallel of Jesus ending in Jerusalem and Paul ending in Rome. Both teaching from the Law and the Prophets concerning the kingdom of God. Jesus deals with religious power thus unlocking a proclamation of transformation for the world.

Essentially nothing has changed since that time. Caesars are no more, yet there are many claimants, personal and corporate to the title of 'lord'. We are still on the same trajectory, making proclamation that all peoples belong to him. I have in my spirit that there is much to be done and brought to a climax back in Jerusalem. Not simply because it is a holy place, but because this Gospel has always been destined to run through the whole earth purifying people and land alike. I believe we are in a major time of acceleration of that process. In the Western world that acceleration means we will see the people of God poured out into the world in ways we have not seen before. Certain church institutions will become more marginal to God's people as the body finds heavenly permission to carry the presence of God with them.

Meanwhile a major shift is to take place in the Muslim world with women at the forefront. And (but not in a exclusive sense) Jerusalem in some way acting as a homing beacon. God is not finished with the Middle East, but the whole world is his, not some square miles in one specific place. So the draw back to Jerusalem will be marked by decentralization where the church has been established, and the raising of the marginalized. This will not be to everyone's liking nor expectation, but is the precursor for waves of his presence to come.

The challenge and critique the prophets gave to Israel was that of 'who is your Protector?' and 'who will be your Provider?' Whenever the nation was judged it was normally over those two core issues. Jesus likewise presented the same challenge to his disciples. He sent them out as 'lambs among wolves'. I can almost hear them say, 'But do you know what wolves love to eat?' So if God did not protect them they would become fodder. Likewise he challenged them over provision: 'Do not take a purse or bag or sandals'. Travel light, and trust God.

In the Western world historically the church has often been favored, having a privileged position. By 2020 much of that will have gone. Why? We are going to find again that he is the Protector and the Provider. There still is more work to be done within the body to prepare for finances to transfer so we will continue see squeeze on ministries financially. Jesus, always the radical, but always the benchmark, in choosing Judas to look after the money was sending a signal for all who follow that people are a higher priority than money.

Finances are coming but the see-saw will swing. Fresh emphases will come on the use of finances. Great entrepreneurs will rise who carry the spirit of humility but have a vision for national transformation. In 1991 I had a vision where those (believers) who handled finance from nations met together and through prayer, wisdom and the prophetic God began to give them strategies for working alongside governments for economic restoration. At a time of economic shaking this is the opportune time. The increase of those with economic expertise who will be working to develop social enterprise in less privileged lands will abound.

Love for a nation is vital and love for a neighborhood must be present for change to take place in that neighborhood, but the love that God is releasing is a global love that has a local outworking. This process is going to bring about a fresh kingdom alignment, and challenge where we simply have national alignments.

There is a work taking place which is of the redeeming from all the nations a people for the King. Great harvests are coming in the places we have not anticipated it. Among the Muslim people a harvest is gathering momentum. Harvest too is coming in the Western world, but the shift he is calling for is an alignment so that we see his harvest field as the world. Days of church restoration of course will continue, but the agenda has shifted. The future shape of the church will be determined by the world. Like water poured out it will find the lowest point, and the pouring out of the people of God is now on us. He has poured into us, he has called us into the river but now there has been a shift. The greatest days ahead are not the days of conferences and within the four walls but the days in the home, the street, the office; the days beyond the four walls.

A running back to the familiar will cause a slowing down of our entrance to the future and leave us with only some nostalgic memories of what used to be. We need to feel insecure, we must feel that if we are to help create a new culture. Not the culture of church, but the culture of the body of Christ continuing to do and to teach what he began (Acts 1:1).

A good working definition of imperial power is that it is marked by a few are empowered who promise benefits to all who comply to the system, but the true benefits flow back to the few. This can take place in a very visible fashion, in say a dictatorial setting, and can also take place in the benign setting of church life. Jesus said of this kind of power that it was not to be 'among you' (Luke 22:25,26). Increasingly this will be judged in all its forms. The future is not the localization of the gifts in a few but the distribution to the many.

The faceless, nameless ones will arise; or rather God's activity through them will only increase. 'Aslan', we read, is not tame. Neither can his followers be tame. The shaking of imperial power means that, even structures that have served thus far, will begin to crumble. The transition to the fresh manifestations will not come neatly and simply through old structures changing. Many new, and even strange things, will begin to emerge outside of apostolic boundaries. That is the nature of the wild-fire of God. Apostles did not shape the work of God in Acts, they were normally a step or two behind what God was doing. He was the boundary breaker and this again will be a hallmark of the next years.

MUSLIM WORLD AND WOMEN

Early in 2009 the Lord spoke to my wife and I to pray for and to watch the women of the Muslim world. He said that they will be a sign that breakthrough is coming, and they will be the means of breakthrough coming. We have been amazed in what has been termed the 'Arab spring' at the vocal presence of women.

A new love for the Muslim world is coming and must come. In the west there has been a (righteous) rising up against the evils done to the unborn, but recently the Lord spoke to my spirit a word that shocked me. He said that when we dehumanize people the end product is the dehumanizing of the life in the womb. The prayer and campaigning about abortion will also have fruit to bear in the love that will come for those of different ethnic backgrounds. Fear will be overcome by love.

AN ECONOMIC WORLD IN CRISIS

Leadership will come forth. Africa is coming into a new season of producing leaders for the coming years. Political and Christian leaders will arise from there, but also Africa will produce leaders who make a serious level of contribution into the banking world. New systems are going to be developed that will not be reliant on current structures and we will see the basis for currency exchange change.

All of this could be very threatening, but it is the environment for the socially-conscious entrepreneurs to rise. Innovation will seem like a gift from heaven that has been unlocked. Problems, even ecological ones such as waste disposal, will be answered with creative responses.

Economically there is a major shift coming. Tighter in the pocket, but more adventurous in spirit will be the result to the people of God. Having less but releasing more. There will come a wave of teaching about stewardship and with it revelation as to the stewardship, not just of the money in one's own account, but the wealth also that is within God's world.

CONFUSION OVER WHO IS FROM GOD

A great phenomenon is going to take place where there will be a number of those like Cyrus who will be 'secular' leaders but anointed by God. Although not believers they will be raised up to carry purposes his purposes forward. They will even at times speak as though they are prophetic voices. This will cause confusion to those who have been taught to look at everything through a Christian lens, rather than seeking to discover the purposes of God.

At the same time though deceitful public figures will

arise. The discernment of those will be necessary. They will often say the same thing as the 'Cyruses', but carry a different spirit. The hallmark that will distinguish the true from the false will be humility. God has been cleansing church leadership of pride, and there is a wave that is coming into the political arena likewise that will humble the prideful. As we see judgments of this take place it will train us in our discernment to know when it is a 'Cyrus' that is speaking.

Likewise there will be those who rise with a spirit of betrayal. Jealousy will mark them. In all of this we are going to learn that we do not look to the 'top' in terms of human position, but that we have to look higher to the One who appoints. We are not to be thrown even when we hear of mainline teachers who are living in compromise. It is the era of the unknown stepping forward who know the Living God and fear him above all else.

Another sign of God at work on the margins will be a number of prisons that will be visited by God, who will come to inmates and staff alike.

WHAT A TIME TO BE ALIVE

A decade of shifts, re-balancing and realignments. A decade for those who walk through the barriers erected by the fear of consequences. The land that God invites us into will always produce good fruit, and that good fruit as always will be guarded by giants. Dependent on who we listen to will make all the difference. Opportunities can be taken or missed for a generation. Fear and a desire for the familiar will rob us, but an adventurous excitement about God's activity will pull us to new heights. The decade will release wholesale changes. We can hold on to what we have and find a diminishing return or sow it into the future.

Martin Scott, carries a passion and great hope for the continent

of Europe, believing that a radical shift within the body of Christ will bring a freedom to express the Gospel beyond the four walls. Since 2009 he has lived with his wife Gayle in Spain where they are seeking to close ancient doors of bondage as they connect with Paul's apostolic prayers for that land, and also find new ways to express the historic testimony to Jesus. He believes the best days are the ones ahead, challenging ones, but ones that will enable / force us to discover the truths of an apostolic Gospel.

website: http://3generations.eu/blog

THE UNSHAKEABLE KINGDOM IN A SHAKABLE WORLD:
KEYS FOR 2012 AND BEYOND

by Stacey Campbell

And His voice shook the earth then, but now He has promised, saying, "YET ONCE MORE I WILL SHAKE NOT ONLY THE EARTH, BUT ALSO THE HEAVEN." This expression, "Yet once more," denotes the removing of those things which can be shaken, as of created things, so that those things which cannot be shaken may remain. Therefore, since we receive a kingdom which cannot be shaken, let us show gratitude, by which we may offer to God an acceptable service with reverence and awe; for our God is a consuming fire. (Hebrews 12:26-29 NASB)

Christians worship a king whose kingdom "is not of this world" (John 18:36). Yet they are to pray that His "kingdom comes . . . on earth" (Matt. 6:10). Jesus told us to pray this prayer because He wants His kingdom to be here "as it is in heaven." Evidently, He believes that prayer will help bring His kingdom to earth. You will note in the two portions of Scripture mentioned above that there are at least two kingdoms: the kingdom of heaven and the kingdom of this world (see also Matt. 4:8; Rev. 11:15; Rev. 12:10). One is shakable; the other is not. It is our joy and privilege to labor with Jesus in actions and prayer so that His unshakable kingdom will come to earth.

Prophets have always seen, and continue to see the clash between the kingdoms. They see the parts that can be shaken (even Jesus Himself spoke of them in Matt. 24). And since prophecy is the testimony of Jesus (Rev. 19:10), it is always redemptive in nature ("And they shall call his name Jesus, for He shall save His people from their sins"). Therefore, whenever true prophecy is in operation, something of the nature of our Savior is being revealed. Even the Old Testament prophets, who prophesied the various judgments of God, only did so in order to try to turn the nation of Israel back to Him. As the book of Jonah illustrates, God's mercy always triumphs over even the prophesied judgments of God. And as the book of Judges illustrates, God uses judgment to bring His own people back to Him. The great prophet Isaiah understood this clearly:

> *At night my soul longs for You, Indeed, my spirit within me seeks You diligently; For when the earth experiences Your judgments, the inhabitants of the world learn righteousness. (Isaiah 26:9)*

Isaiah's longing for God produced in Him the understanding that God's judgments would produce righteousness on the earth. Today our world is in desperate need of righteousness, and judgment and discipline are used by God to turn nations back to Himself whenever they have veered off course.

A cursory reading of any daily headline will be ample illustration for how far a nation is from the will of God. Obviously, great alignment is needed between heaven and earth, between the nations and God. And so shakings are here and they are coming, not for destruction, but for purification . . . to bring people back to dependence on God, and ultimately to prepare the earth for His return and the fullness of His kingdom to be established.

2012 and beyond, depending one's vantage point, will be either great or terrible (Joel 2:11; cf Acts 2:20). The global economic crisis has only begun. Increasingly, there will be a divide in the Western world between the rich and the poor and the middle class will be hit the hardest. The economic center of the earth will continue to shift, as the US loses its stronghold on the global marketplace. The stance of Islam and its commitment to worldwide dominance over all other world religions will manifest in violence and more tumult the Middle East. Only a prayer life commensurate to the prayer life of the Muslims will defeat its advance into Western nations. If the Church does not pray, the Christian nations will not be able to withstand the agenda of the Muslim advance. The war of terrorism is ultimately a war in the spirit, which only will be won through prayer. The spirit of the great prophet Elijah, a man just like us ("but he prayed"), must come upon the Christians who desire to keep their nations moored to the Christian foundations of their forefathers.

In September 2009, I was in Europe on the last day of Ramadan, which also happened to be the first day of Rosh Hashanah that year. These two spiritual calendars do not always coincide like that, but on that day, I clearly heard the Lord say, "It is the calm before the storm." Let me unpack what I understood Him to be saying by that. He caused me to understand that there would be a period of relative calm, but that soon there would be great storms in the Middle East, as spiritual calendars of Islam and Israel collided. From the first month of 2011, the whole world has watched the storms in the Islamic nations break out . . . and there is more to come.

What I felt prophetically is that these storms have the potential to escalate into national military threats between Middle Eastern nations (particularly Iran) and Israel. We have already seen, from the beginning of 2011, the tumult of the Muslim nations. They are in upheaval, setting the stage for either greater freedom or greater terror. Spiritual calendars are colliding. The increasing economic pressures will also be a factor in drawing nations into military alliances. The polarities of the religious ideologies will manifest, not simply in terrorism, but in national military initiatives. Today we are in a time when all believers must really pray for the peace of Jerusalem like never before.

SO WHAT IS THE CHURCH TO DO?

Isaiah 40 is a key Scripture for this hour of human history. For myself, it is a Scripture which brought about great personal alignment in my heart, as one of the greatest visitations of my life occurred when I was 18 years old, while praying Isaiah 40 in my university dorm room one evening. At that time, my whole room lit up with a golden glow and I had an out-of-body experience where the Lord showed me His sovereignty over all the nations (even nations in war and conflict) . . . and over my own life as well. I heard His audible voice saying, "I am Lord of the nations. And I am Lord of you. . . ." and He gave me specific instructions that would change the course of my life. My entire future was set in motion from that one experience. I experienced what I will call "a theo-centric shift," meaning that from that experience, I understood that my life was not my own; rather, I was created for a divine destiny, before-ordained by God Himself (Ephesians 2:10).

I have recently been meditating on Isaiah 40 again, and the Lord has been speaking to me about a great shift coming to the Body of Christ. It will be a theo-centric shift, where the world will understand the sovereignty of God over all the nations. As Isaiah 40 clearly points out, God is Lord of the nations. In fact, they are a "drop in the bucket to Him . . . less than nothing and meaningless" (Isaiah 40: 15-17). John the Baptist quoted Isaiah 40 as he prepared Israel for the first coming of the Messiah. At this time, there was a shift of heart and focus proclaimed by the "voice in the wilderness."

Once again, Isaiah 40 is an important a key Scripture for the time that is unfolding on the earth. When natural, economic, and national shakings break out over the earth, we must understand that God is Lord of the nations. He is sovereign over every nation, and He is ultimately making the wrong things right.

A voice is calling,

Clear the way for the LORD in the wilderness;
Make smooth in the desert a highway for our God.
Let every valley be lifted up,
And every mountain and hill be made low;
And let the rough ground become a plain,
And the rugged terrain a broad valley;
Then the glory of the LORD will be revealed,
And all flesh will see it together;
For the mouth of the LORD has spoken.

(Isaiah 40: 3-5)

The prophets through the direction of God state that God is Lord of the nations, and He is Lord of His Church. An honest assessment of the earth shows that this is not a reality right now. Therefore for the world to come into alignment of what God, through His prophets, has said will be the earth's future reality, a number of things will be changing. There will be a preparation of the earth itself before His return. Mountains will be made low and rough ground will become a plain. There will also be a great shift in the nations where He will cause those who know Him not to fear, but to say, "Here is your God."

Get yourself up on a high mountain,
O Zion, bearer of good news,
Lift up your voice mightily,
O Jerusalem, bearer of good news;
Lift it up, do not fear
Say to the cities of Judah,
"Here is your God!"
Behold, the Lord GOD will come with might,
With His arm ruling for Him
Behold, His reward is with Him
And His recompense before Him. (Isaiah 40: 9-10)

As God deals with the nations of the earth in an

intensified way, the earth will understand that "The Lord, he is God!" (1 Kings 18:39). "The earth is the Lord's and the fullness thereof." (Psalm 24:1). He is sovereign over all that is coming – and He knows what is coming.

There is such good news in this reality! The best is yet to come! When God prophesied through the major prophets in the Old Testament about the coming Babylonian invasion, He also gave them the solution and the understanding of what to do for the season of discipline and purification. They were to go peacefully, to build houses and settle in Babylon (Jeremiah 29:5ff, 28). He gave them instruction how to overcome when the judgment came. As cited above, judgments from God are meant to teach the world righteousness. Yet once more, judgment – godly judgment – is coming to our world to bring us to righteousness. The answer of how to endure and overcome is the most important thing to understand for 2012 and beyond.

SO WHAT CAN WE DO?

All over the world believers who know the nature of God are responding to the sound of judgment with a cry for mercy. This cry is coming from the exploding global prayer movement. But more prayer is needed. The coming hour will necessitate that the entire spectrum of global Christianity must change. A new wineskin! The great wineskin shift for this hour of church history will be from an ego-centric model (seeker-sensitive, equipping-oriented, geared to people), to a theo-centric model (the Father's house, with ministry to the Lord Himself). Then, as we stare deeply into the face of God, we will be overcomers in the coming season (Revelation 12:11).

For mercy to triumph over judgment, we will need to change in the way we do church, returning to the biblical understanding that God's house is a "house of prayer"

(Matthew 21:13; Mark 11:17; Luke 19:46). The 'called out ones' (ecclesia) are to be theo-centric in their orientation. I believe that unless we build God's house as a house of prayer, the Church will not have the spiritual strength to overcome in the increased shakings we are about to endure. Rather, we will be like many of the disciples in Jesus' day, who "withdrew and followed Him no more" (John 6:66).

The house of prayer is the house that the Father chose for Himself ("My House will be a house of prayer . . ." Isaiah 56), and it is the wineskin that will bring in the nations (it's purpose has always been ". . . for all nations"). Like the tabernacle of David, it is birthed "so that the rest of mankind may seek the Lord." (Acts 15:16). As the God of the nations, clears the way by leveling the high places and raising the low places, earth must come in alignment with all that He has revealed about Himself and His ultimate purpose for the earth. Those who experience a "theo-centric shift," by seeking Him in regular, consistent prayer, will understand that these coming shakings are part of the great preparation of the earth and its people for the return of Jesus.

The good news is that though these shaking will come, there will be justice for all, especially Israel, as a result of these shakings.

Why do you say, O Jacob, and assert, O Israel,
"My way is hidden from the LORD,
And the justice due me escapes the notice of my God"?

Today, God is accelerating events and collisions to accomplish global justice. It may not look like what we expected, but God will bring justice none-the-less. Our part is to seek Him, to wait on Him for strength to endure and overcome. The need of the hour is for revelation on how to co-labor with Him as the kingdom(s) of this world become(s) the kingdom(s) of our Lord and His Christ (Revelations 11:15).

Do you not know? Have you not heard? The Everlasting God, the LORD,
the Creator of the ends of the earth
Does not become weary or tired
His understanding is inscrutable.
He gives strength to the weary,
And to him who lacks might He increases power.
Though youths grow weary and tired,
And vigorous young men stumble badly,
Yet those who wait for the LORD
Will gain new strength;
They will mount up with wings like eagles,
They will run and not get tired,
They will walk and not become weary (Isaiah 40:28-31)

I encourage you to meditate on this Scripture and call the Church to pray. The theo-centric shift of a praying Church will also ensure that God's people are filled with faith when shakings occur. Because we understand that our kingdom is unshakable, Christians will realize that it is our mandate and responsibility to preach the unshakable kingdom wherever the shakings occur. Shakings, when seen through the eyes of faith, will cause the people of God to rush towards the giant when the world is retreating in fear and confusion. We proclaim, manifest, and bring the kingdom of God to every arena that is shaking. We pray and co-labor with Jesus until God's economy, God's life, God's power, God's healing, God's character – the fullness of God's kingdom comes to the world. Expect that those who have insight will use the opportunities created by shakings to lead many to righteousness. Already God is positioning his modern-day Josephs, Daniel's, and Pauls to take leadership in strategic worldly kingdoms of government, economy, arts and entertainment, sports, etc.... They are positioned there by God Himself. His kingdom is coming and with it His justice, His mercy and the revelation of His dominion and preeminence in all things.

Finally, Acts 2 and Joel 2 give us great clues about how God intends to deal with nations. He says: "there will be signs in the heavens and signs on the earth . . . blood, fire and billows of smoke . . . and everyone who calls on the name of the Lord shall be saved." He knows what is coming. He will shake the heavens and the earth – earthquakes and wars and rumours of war (Matt. 24:6-14) will be the backdrop for one of the greatest harvests the world has ever seen (Revelations 7:9-14).

A primary fruit of this theo-centric shift that has already begun is the re-emergence of miracles of biblical proportions. As the understanding of gazing at God increases through prayer, so will the miracles that intimacy with God produces (Philippians 3:10). True knowledge of God is experiential, not mental assent. Transformation occurs when we stare at God (2 Corinthians 3:18)– we become like Him, partakers of His divine nature (1 Peter 1:4 NASB). The power that raised Jesus from the dead will become manifest in the daily lives of the disciples of Jesus, resulting in extraordinary miracles occurring through "average" believers. Believers will model what knowing God looks like in holiness, lowliness, and power.

For 2012 and beyond a new wineskin is emerging: the house of prayer, producing victorious faith, incredible wisdom (Daniel 12:3,10) and a release of supernatural power unto an accelerated harvest of nations in the midst of judgment. The things that can be shaken will continue to be shaken so that the things that cannot be shaken will remain. What comfort to know that we are part of an unshakeable kingdom! Nothing in it can be shaken. A glorious, victorious, beautiful Bride will show forth the nature of Her Bridegroom. She will model His love and compassion by going to the poor, the broken, and the bewildered in the midst of shakings. She will display wisdom when none of the wicked understand (Daniel 12:10). When the nations shake in fear, the Church will model the unshakeable kingdom of God in love and power. And multitudes will turn to Jesus, satisfying His desire that we all will be with Him where He is (John 17:24 NASB).

Stacey Campbell and her husband Wesley, are authors and founders of New Life Church in Kelowna, B.C., Revival Now Ministries, Eyes & Wings School of Supernatural Ministry, and an international outreach to orphans called Be a Hero.

www.revivalnow.com

www.beahero.org

HOPE REFORMATION:
HOPE IS COMING FORTH IN 2010-2020
THROUGH HOPE REFORMERS

by Bob Hartley

I have had a repeated dream over the years where God was giving churches, businesses, and cities a new name as in Isaiah 62, and they were renamed HOPE. In these dreams, God showed me that the Body of Christ has been secured in love from their salvation experiences, but now He is bringing forth hope to the Body of Christ that advances the heart! Without hope, it's easy to hide in the back room and say, "Jesus, it's not working on the planet, come back!" But with a hopeful heart, we are enabled to go after abundant life in this hour and have something to offer the Son of God when He returns!

There is an Isaiah 45 reality coming forth, where He is bringing forth hidden treasures of His nature that have been buried for thousands of years! "I will give you the treasures of darkness and hidden wealth of secret places, so that you may know that it is I, the LORD, the God of Israel, who calls you by your name."

THE ENCOUNTER: HOPE REFORMATION FOR 2010-2020

Recently, I began to ask Him about the next 10 years, and here is what He began to speak. He was trumpeting a message of miracles and of a Hope Reformation, and He declared that 2010 would be a year that the Father's heart secures people in His love, and the Father's voice, through decrees, would advance people and nations into their God-ordained destinies. These decrees would help give the Church back its courage and hope!

The Lord showed me that beginning in 2010 and continuing through the next 10 years, He is raising up Patriarchs and Matriarchs of every age that will decree what the Lord is saying, and they will decree another future for the Body of Christ. Job 22:28 says that if you decree a thing it will happen, if you are in agreement with Him. "You will also decree a thing, and it will be established for you; and light will shine on your ways." He is raising up mothers and fathers in the Spirit, for as Paul said in 1 Corinthians 4:15, "For though you might have ten thousand instructors in Christ, yet you do not have many fathers."

THE DECREES OF THE FATHER'S VOICE FOR 2010-2020

The first decree that the Lord told me at His table was that "Hope is Coming Forth in 2010 through Hope Reformers." He showed me these Hope Reformers who had a third perspective-not a perspective of the world or of their own soul, but Heaven's perspective. These Hope Reformers had abandoned that which is evil and full of despair and had returned to an appropriate, godly and hope- filled state. He showed me a picture of Joshua and Caleb from Numbers 13:25-33, where they looked at the Promised Land and they had hope that surely the children of God could take the land despite the giants there-because our God is greater! Their perspective was an appropriate, godly and hope-filled perspective, not one of doubt, fear and despair that magnifies the challenges above our great and awesome God. NO! We can take the land! I saw that these Hope Reformers are the "arise and shine" ones of Isaiah 60:1, and they were coming forth with the Father's voice of hope this year.

The second decree that the Lord told me was that "Hopeful prophets would come forth in 2010." These Hope

Reformers will be like the farmers in Zechariah 13:4-5 that are prophetic builders who plant a seed and then trust that the seed will bring forth a fruitful harvest. I saw the Father speak to these sons and daughters about cities whose architect and maker is God, with His patriarchal voice that is able to see a very long way out and build accordingly by decreeing hopeful realities and a hopeful future. It doesn't negate the challenges, but sees the "Greater than" God, as in Deuteronomy 7:17-18, "If you should say in your heart, 'These nations are greater than I; how can I dispossess them?' you shall not be afraid of them; you shall well remember what the LORD your God did to Pharaoh and to all Egypt." He showed me that incomplete prophecy is seeing the challenges without an answer in Him. He said that you cannot build off of the negative. He showed me that He is a truthful, positive, confident God who is summing all things up in His Son.

The third decree that the Lord told me at His table was that He would bring forth a "Clear trumpet sound in 2010" that would emphasize that there is a Hope Reformation coming forth that is not just about a distant eternal security, though that is our anchor; it is a reformation called living in hope for today. It's about the nature of God being expressed as the hopeful God who will bring forth that Joshua eyesight, where the Body of Christ stands and decrees, "We can take the land!"

These are the decrees that the Lord showed me, that He has laid out for the Body of Christ as we move forward here in 2010 to 2020.

THE LORD DECREED FOR 2010 TO 2020: "I HAVE A ROYAL JOURNEY OF HOPE TO BRING THE BODY OF CHRIST INTO THIS HOPE REFORMATION"

The Father began to share with me the decrees that were key to get these Hope Reformers prepared to deliver His decrees to the nations of the earth. He decreed that there is a royal path and a journey to equip the Hope Reformers for the times and seasons we are in. He told me that there has always been a house of our pilgrimage, an ancient path, and a good way for us during a particular time on the planet that God is endorsing, as in Jeremiah 6:16; "This is what the LORD says: 'Stand at the crossroads and look; ask for the ancient paths, ask where the good way is, and walk in it, and you will find rest for your souls...'"

He showed me a royal journey that the Body of Christ is to go on together, and He called it the Royal Journey of Hope. I saw 50 million people that would go on this royal journey of hope. They'd go into cities, nations and businesses, and they'd be able to move them out of despair and into hope, where they advance into a future with a great harvest.

THEN THE LORD DECREED FOR 2010 TO 2020: "GO ON THIS JOURNEY AND LEARN FIVE LESSONS OF HOPE TO BECOME A FORTRESS OF HOPE"

I've had recurring dreams of people that would be in a classroom in Heaven where they were to learn five lessons of hope, and they would graduate those lessons and become coronated as Hope Reformers. Then they would be sent out of that heavenly place with such a certainty that they would speak into the clouds, and the clouds would then rain over geographical areas.

Everywhere it would rain, everyone would get wet with hope! I saw great hopers coming forth like Winston Churchill and Hans Nielsen Hauge, and they came forth with a message of hope in God, and were not altered or moved by the circumstances and challenges of the day; instead, they changed the circumstances and challenges of the day through the force of hope in God that brought forth a hopeful future for others.

I saw these Hope Reformers moving up five rows in this classroom as they learned these lessons of hope. The first lesson was "Hope in God," where they encountered Him as the "God who is enough for every life situation."

After these things the word of the Lord came to Abram in a vision, saying, "Do not be afraid, Abram. I am your shield, your exceedingly great reward." Genesis 15:1

The second lesson was "Hope in People," where they encountered Him as the "Redeemer and Good Shepherd," and they received a "new view of people," where they developed a great hope in God's ability to redeem and love themselves and others. I saw that there had been so much disappointment toward other human beings, where the lens that life has been looked through has been critical analysis and evaluation, but I saw a hopeful appreciative lens come forth as this lesson was learned.

I will praise You, for I am fearfully and wonderfully made; marvelous are Your works, and that my soul knows very well. Psalm 139:14 (This is appreciation not only for ourselves but for others.)

The third lesson was "Hope in the Next Generation," where they encountered God as the "Patriarch and Fiercely Dedicated Father." When they received this revelation, God opened up hope for the next generation, renaming them "Generation Hope," not "Generation X-Y-Z," and they began to see the next generation as beautiful, and as a blessing.

But Jesus said, "Let the little children come to Me, and do not forbid them; for of such is the Kingdom of Heaven." Matthew 19:14

The fourth lesson was "Hope in Prayer," where they encountered Him as the "Great Communicator and One who Answers Prayer." When they received this revelation, they would receive a "new seeing," where they would be able to see out a very long way, like Abraham seeing Jesus' day. They would always build on their knees!

Call to Me, and I will answer you, and show you great and mighty things, which you do not know. Jeremiah 33:3

The fifth lesson was "Hope in Cities and Nations," where they encountered Him as the "Benevolent King of the Nations." When they received this revelation, a force of hope for geographical areas would come forth, and they saw the burning desire in the Lord's heart for cities and nations that would love Him well. I saw a new generation coming forth that will have hope for cities and nations set into their DNA code, and they will be our bank accounts, where they have a confidence in God that is unpolluted; and they would be like Solomons who didn't have to fight the wars that David fought, but they will be wise ones who will be able to rule and believe for a whole community and a whole area.

Ask of Me, and I will give You the nations for Your inheritance, and the ends of the earth for Your possession. Psalm 2:8

THEN THE LORD DECREED FOR 2010 TO 2020: "I AM ENABLING YOU (HOPE REFORMERS) TO HELP PRESENT ME WITH CITIES AND NATIONS THAT WILL LOVE ME WELL AND HOPE IN ME."

Specifically for 2010, it is a year of great harvest, and there will be seven nations that could experience storms of different types. These storms are not specifically geophysical, but they could be financial, political, etc. Right after He spoke this, Haiti had a real storm. I don't believe these storms are just going to be literal catastrophes; I am not a prophet of catastrophe, but for example, in Greece, there will be financial storm. But the Father has an answer! There will be the Hope Reformers of the Father's voice that have that personal devotion with Him; and they will come out with public decrees with a certainty, so that they can affect these nations and key people in the nations appropriately, so they can influence people and put their hand into Jesus' hand, in those hours of challenge.

Jesus said: "First, I want to show you what I am doing across the earth. I began to tell you in 1983 that I desire to establish cities and nations that would love Me well and hope in Me, as in Revelation 19:10, with the testimony of Jesus, where Jesus could enter in to the different arenas of life and not be lonely there, but be received and loved well there."

In 1983, I had been asking the Lord day and night, "God, what is on Your heart?" and in an open vision in a stairwell in Fort Collins, the Lord showed me several progressive pictures. I saw how Jesus had been mostly unperceived in cities across the earth, in the midst of the day and the arenas of life, like politics, education, social arenas, the arts, families, and the marketplace. The Lord shared how He desired to see His name vindicated as in Ezekiel 36:23, and how His heart burned to see cities and nations come forth that would love Him well and would receive His love and hope in Him.

"I will show the holiness of My great name, which has been profaned among the nations, the name you have profaned among them. Then the nations will know that I am the LORD", declares the Sovereign LORD, "when I show Myself holy through you before their eyes." Ezekiel 36:23

Since 1983, I have met many of the Hope Reformers that I saw in that original vision, because they were real people and real places, and these ones are transforming their cities and nations to be those places that love Him well. It is happening!

THEN THE LORD DECREED FOR 2010 TO 2020: "I AM CHANGING THE NATURE OF CHRISTIANITY TO HOPEFUL CHRISTIANITY"

The Scout showed me that the Body of Christ had often been sitting in the back room, staring at fears, but then I saw them move through a door into the radiant hope for the day and for the future in God in 2010. I saw that the Body of Christ was ready to advance and take territory as they helped to bring forth the celebration of Jesus all over the cities and nations of the earth. I saw it happening in businesses and families, like the Acts 2 community of Believers, and I was so touched that I cried and cried, and then I began to cry out for this reality.

He showed me that Hope is not an abstract word! Hope is confident expectation, appropriately, in our God. If you get a hopeful son or daughter, they smile at their future. If you get a hopeful Christianity, they smile at their future, and they bring forth a great harvest. Sheep will become warhorses through this process of hope, and they won't even recognize themselves!

He showed me the little areas, the little foxes of Song of Solomon 2:15 that pollute our hope. But He had an answer for us: everyone in this blueprint was to get a hope journal. When they would start to feel that distaste of hopelessness when they looked at another person, maybe impatience or frustration, they would go right to their journal, and take the hope promise and attack that area. This way they avoided becoming like Gulliver, who was strapped down by "little problems."

I dreamed of what people looked like with radiant hope! It was the Daniel 12:3 reality, "Those who are wise will shine like the brightness of the heavens, and those who lead many to righteousness, like the stars forever and ever." We are going to see the great lights come forth. That little dismal area and secret place in our hearts where we don't go, and where we have hopelessness, He is going to meet it with His nature in hope!

THEN THE LORD DECREED FOR 2010 TO 2020: "THERE

WILL BE HOLY, HOPEFUL ALLIANCES AND 'MARRIAGES MADE IN HEAVEN' THIS YEAR"

There are great lights that are to come together this year and help support one another. The Scout showed me that God is raising up Hope Reformers through right marriages, marriages made in Heaven, causing the right ministries to come together to bring forth the public decrees and plans from the Lord to help these nations. There will be sheep nations that will come forth this year. The Scout also gave a warning, that if ones go into nations in which they are not sent, premature spiritual or physical death could occur, because they will be trespassing the land and walking outside of the blessing of the Lord. These ones MUST be sent!

WHAT IS YOUR PART?

Your part is to see this Journey of Hope that the Lord is bringing us on in 2010 to 2020. He is taking us into this Hope Room where we meet and decree a face of God, where we start to walk out the day as Hope Reformers, confessing and living out who He is, and then we decree His voice in hope. I believe many reading this article are called to be these Hope Reformers, those who move into the force of Hope in God through adoration and devotion, who will hear the Father's voice in hope and will release decrees over nations and the Body of Christ for this hour.

Get on the journey of hope!

Bob Hartley is the founder of Hartley Institute/Deeper Waters Ministry in Kansas City, Missouri.
http://www.bobhartley.org

WHO IS LEADING US THROUGH THE TIMES AHEAD? YOU!

By Paul Keith Davis

The eyes of the Lord are roving to and fro looking for a righteous agency on the earth to stand in the gap. The Lord is asking, "Is there no man when I call? Is there anyone to answer? I am speaking is there anyone listening? Is my hand shortened at all that it cannot redeem? Or have I no power to deliver? Don't you know who I am?"

There will be a remnant of people on the earth who hear and respond to this call. According to Isaiah 50:2 the Lord asked:

> *Why was there no man when I came? When I called, why was there no one to answer? Is My hand so short that it cannot ransom? Or have I no power to deliver? Behold, I dry up the sea with My rebuke, I make the rivers a wilderness; their fish stink for lack of water and die of thirst.*

God's Spirit can change things quickly. He is giving His people an instructed tongue that we may sustain the weary with a word from Him. He is presently awakening many saints morning by morning that He may give to them eyes to see and ears to hear instruction like His disciples.

The righteous prayer of Job intervened for those around him despite their folly.

It is time the fortune of God's people be restored as well. The Lord turned the captivity of Job and restored double when he prayed for his friends. We are entering the season of the double-portion.

For I will accept him so that I may not do with you according to your folly, because you have not spoken of Me what is right, as My servant Job has...The LORD restored the fortunes of Job when he prayed for his friends, and the LORD increased all that Job had twofold. (Job 42:8 & 10)

Many in the Church are coming to the end of a time of pruning and judgment as it is beginning in the world. God's desire is for our light to shine brightly as many people head our way in this dark season. It is time for those who overcome to arise with a measure of His glory resting upon them. This will literally be the fulfillment of Daniel's prophecy when he wrote:

Those who have insight will shine brightly like the brightness of the expanse of heaven, and those who lead the many to righteousness, like the stars forever and ever. Daniel 12:3

It is time for the accomplishment of divine purposes and a wave of harvest. The Lord is laying claim to this generation of young people as well as the seasoned and mature. It will be both the Joshua's and the Caleb's. The Lord is healing the fracture He has created in a third day harvest of the wounded and persecuted. His will is being accomplished in a mighty way so that a harvest can be achieved.

Trials in the earth will increase while at the same time end-time truths from the book of Revelations become increasingly clear. Great understanding will be delegated to the Church concerning these mysteries. The book of Revelations is a love letter to the Lord's bride and prepares her to be joined to Him.

DESTINED FOR VICTORY

The Lord has already triumphed over the adversary and

made a public spectacle of him. Many in a First-Fruits harvest will comprehend that reality more fully and appropriate it. The Lord delegates His victory to us when we are joined to Him.

One of our greatest callings in this hour is to no longer be considered the Lord's servants, but His friends. We have a Friend who is eternally positioned on His throne of victory and authority and we need a more complete vision of this to fully activate our faith. Commissioning from the Throne Room can be a living reality as promised through God's word. He is saying, "Come up here!"

The Lord's Church is required to discern the times and seasons and possess the mind of Christ for this day. It isn't His desire to hide it from us, but reveal great understanding so that the worldly may see God's blessing and wisdom upon His people. That is what the grooming of the last decade has been intended to accomplish. The pain of our past is the preparation for our future.

Brokenness without the spirit of understanding breeds hopelessness; but brokenness with understanding imparts the hope of our calling in God. The Lord's Spirit has been pruning and uprooting our fallen nature and carnal plans in order to inject His own pure nature. His ultimate purpose is to reveal the Fatherhood of God and make us His mature sons and daughters.

Though it seems we have failed in many ways, these years have actually cultivated humility in many. The arm of the flesh and our own strength cannot accomplish the end-time mandate. It will not be by the might of man nor the power of our own ingenuity; but by His Spirit alone. Our job is to yield and learn to co-operate with Him.

Like Jacob, the Lord has destroyed our dependence upon human strength and changed our nature. A new name is being given according to Revelations 2:17 to those who overcome in this fashion.

"A Redeemer will come to Zion, and to those who turn from transgression in Jacob," declares the LORD. "As for me, this is My covenant with them," says the LORD: "My Spirit which is upon you, and My words which I have put in your mouth shall not depart from your mouth, nor from the mouth of your offspring, nor from the mouth of your offspring's offspring," says the LORD, "from now and forever." Isaiah 59:20-21

THE LATTER GLORY

Sometimes the greatest prophecies come in the midst of the most unlikely circumstances. Following Israel's Babylonian captivity, the remnant that saw the majesty and splendor of Solomon's Temple likely found it difficult to believe Haggai's prophecy when he said:

Speak now to Zerubbabel the son of Shealtiel, governor of Judah, and to Joshua the son of Jehozadak, the high priest, and to the remnant of the people saying, "Who is left among you who saw this temple in its former glory? And how do you see it now? Does it not seem to you like nothing in comparison?

But now take courage, Zerubbabel,' declares the LORD, "take courage also, Joshua son of Jehozadak, the high priest, and all you people of the land take courage,' declares the LORD, "and work; for I am with you,' declares the LORD of hosts.

As for the promise which I made you when you came out of Egypt, My Spirit is abiding in your midst; do not fear!' For thus says the LORD of hosts, "Once more in a little while, I am going to shake the heavens and the earth, the sea also and the dry land.

I will shake all the nations; and they will come with the wealth of all nations, and I will fill this house with glory,' says the LORD of hosts. The silver is Mine and the gold is Mine,' declares the LORD of hosts. The latter glory of this house will be greater than the former,' says the LORD of hosts, "and in this place I will give peace,' declares the LORD of hosts." Haggai 2:2-9

Nothing before or since has ever compared to the wonder of Solomon's Temple. Even so, this incredible prophecy points to a time of extraordinary restoration and promise. Today many still find it difficult to believe that the glory of this latter-day house will exceed the glory of the early apostolic church. Nevertheless, God has promised it and His Spirit will see it fulfilled.

God WILL Tabernacle in a body of people in these last days to exhibit His holy character and do exploits that will exceed any previously demonstrated in human history. We must begin to gear up for this reality, at least in part by understanding God's dealings with prior champions.

THE MAID OF ORLEANS

I have been fascinated by the life of Joan of Arc. After reading Mark Twain's incredible book on her life, I felt its truth was pertinent to this present transition season. We are entering a time when the deposit of God's Spirit that rested upon prior great champions will be reinstituted on those who have been prepared for them. This will be a first-fruits harvest that will provoke the body forward into a season of great harvest.

There are very valuable Kingdom principles that we can learn from the life of this wonderful prophetess. Her courage, valor and obedience will typify many in this last days generation who will give themselves totally to God's plan and purpose. I trust this article is a blessing to you.

Few women in history are as intriguing as Jeanne D'Arc, the French peasant girl born in 1412, who heard and obeyed heaven. To some she was a saint, to others a heretic, but history chronicles her as emerging from obscurity to become her nation's youngest military leader.

In 15 months she changed the course of European

history. Her eventual martyrdom was Satan's attempt to destroy her divine gift, but that same impartation can be inherited by today's "Joan of Arcs" through God's divine justice.

A SUPERNATURAL VOICE

For her, the unlikely destiny began one summer afternoon at the age of 13. On that fateful day she saw a brilliant light and heard the audible voice of the Archangel Michael, leader of God's armies.

Michael addressed her as "Joan the Maid" with the added admonition to live a pure and virtuous life. He announced her destiny as a God appointed deliverer to lead the army of France. Joan reported, "I recognized that it was the voice of an angel. This voice has always guarded me well and I have always understood it; it instructed me to be good and to go to church often."

To Joan, the voices of God's spiritual messengers could be distinguished in the same fashion as one person communicates with another. She received audible expressions from the spiritual realm that charged her with the formidable task of uniting a fragmented army and altering the fate and leadership of her nation.

A DELIVERER IS BORN

The extreme hardship of one hundred years of war with England preceded the appearance of Joan. The English occupied considerable portions of France with plans of further expansion until the prophetess shifted the momentum to the French.

The messengers of Heaven conveyed to her a twofold commission: first, to lead an army against the English in defense of Orleans, a crucial and strategic city for the French;

and secondly, to restore the throne to its rightful heir, the Dauphin of France, a term used to identify the heir apparent who later became Charles VII. France had not had a crowned king since the death of Charles VI in 1422. Instead, the French crown had passed to the infant king Henry VI of England through a treaty signed by Charles VI.

This twofold mandate was an unthinkable task for an illiterate teenager living in the 15th century. Even so, the messengers from Heaven gave explicit directions. Joan possessed the uncanny willingness to risk life and limb in obedience to their instructions. She relinquished herself totally to the cause of Heaven that launched her into this supernatural arena.

THE MANDATE ESTABLISHED

To share this vision with the Dauphin of France, Joan journeyed over 300 miles through enemy territory for her first encounter with Charles VII. Charles actually staged a test to determine the authenticity her revelations.

When Joan entered the huge meeting hall filled with over 300 guests the Dauphin was not seated on his throne. Instead, he was dressed as a commoner and had mingled with the crowd. Led by her supernatural Council, Joan walked directly to Charles and addressed him as the imminent leader of France. Moreover, she also divulged divine insight involving his life known only to he and God. This validated for the eventual king that Joan of Arc was no ordinary maiden.

Subsequently, Charles and his councilmen embraced her vision and allowed her to lead 4000 troops in support of the besieged city of Orleans on April 29, 1429. The victory was swift and sure!

After capturing smaller forts that bordered Orleans, Joan surrounded the occupied city and led the assault against the English. Joan was gravely wounded in the conflict, as she had earlier predicted. Nevertheless, by the end of the day she returned to the battle. The mere sight of their courageous leader rallied the French army who promptly routed the remaining English forces. So moved were these hardened soldiers by Joan's anointing and heroism that they "gave up swearing and prostitutes and committed themselves to a virtuous life."

Joan insisted the men under her charge conduct themselves in a manner becoming professional soldiers. She allowed no swearing or lewd behavior and expected commendable character. The men willingly followed her leadership and affectionately bestowed on her the title "maid of Orleans."

In subsequent weeks, several other French cities enduring English occupation were liberated by Joan and her army. So convincing were the early victories that in one confrontation only three French soldiers perished compared to over 2000 English casualties.

After accepting the surrender of Troyes, Joan persuaded Charles to return to Rheims for his royal coronation. In fulfillment of Joan's directive given by the Lord through Heavenly messengers, CharlesVII was officially recognized as monarch of France.

HER BETRAYAL AND DEATH

Despite her conquests, betrayal from French leaders led to Joan's capture; this too according to her own predictions. In embarrassment, English rulers determined to prove her success resulted from witchcraft and sorcery. They added to her charges heresy—the act of challenging the authority of the Church. The representatives of the Church who tried her believed God spoke only to priests. It flew is the face of their belief system for God to communicate directly with individuals.

For nearly five months Joan of Arc was imprisoned, not in a facility for women but with English soldiers. Nevertheless, strengthened by the Lord and His Heavenly messengers, she remained steadfast throughout the ordeal.

To validate the charge of heresy, the English employed clergyman and theologians who strenuously examined Joan with the malice intent of discrediting her testimony. Remarkably, her wise and skillful answers alleviated their entrapping questions. According to Joan, Heavenly messengers regularly brought to her God's perfect council.

Ultimately, the tainted court rendered a guilty verdict and condemned Joan to be burned at the stake. At 9 a.m. on May 30, 1431 the 19-year-old messenger of God was wrongfully executed. As the flames began to consume her body, a cross held before her eyes was Joan's sole request. Her final word was the name Jesus.

Five hundred years after being burned at the stake for heresy, Joan of Arc is declared a saint and revered by the country she saved.

A CALL FOR JUSTICE

The loving eyes of our Heavenly Judge see and record every action of humanity. In this end-time generation the books of Heaven will be opened and restitution offered for injustices committed against God's covenant people.

As with Joan of Arc, Satan has battled the saints of God for millennia and seemingly prevailed. Nevertheless, God, as the Righteous Judge, will render a final verdict on behalf of the saints. Daniel recorded:

> *I kept looking, and that horn was waging war with the saints an overpowering them until the Ancient of Days came and judgment was passed in favor of the saints of the Highest One, and the time arrived when the saints took possession of the kingdom.* -Daniel 7:21-22

Divine justice, released in this age, will be a key to empower God's people. Joan of Arc's life was a prophetic model. There will be many who follow her standard with faithful and obedient hearts and commissioned in awesome ways. Every seemingly lost commission, anointing, and spiritual gift will be redeemed and released to willing candidates.

For thousands of years God's children have been martyred, persecuted, and plundered, but Heavenly justice will decree that all be fully restored and compensated. All things take place under the all-seeing eye of God, and He has promised to restore all that our adversary has ruined. Clearly Joan and others like her, received a martyr's reward in eternity. Moreover, they sowed spiritual seeds that will reap the most outstanding deposit of divine grace never before demonstrated.

I WILL RESTORE

The Joel 2:25 promise of restoration is one of the paramount passages of this day. God pledges:

> *I will restore to you the years that the swarming locust has eaten, The crawling locust, The consuming locust, And the chewing locust, My great army which I sent among you.* -Joel 2:25

Joan of Arc was God's appointed representative during a crucial juncture in human history. Abuse of authority from corrupt political officials eradicated the Heavenly deposit entrusted to her. God's just nature will mandate a manifold restoration of this and other lost anointing through faithful and obedient vessels prepared to apprehend and demonstrate this destiny and the Lord's redemptive virtues.

Paul Keith and Wanda Davis are the founders of WhiteDove Ministries. www.whitedoveministries.org.

COMPANY 81

By Charlie Shamp

I believe that 2012 will be the marking of a new era in Church History where many in the Body of Christ will go where no generation has gone before. It is high time that we let the past be the past. This will truly be an unprecedented time to press toward the unseen realms of the glory of God and embrace the places that God is calling us to go as the Body of Christ. There have been many mighty revivalists and miracle workers who moved in spectacular Kingdom power and glory in the past, but what they did and encountered in God has only lead us to aim much higher in our generation. They have paved a way to the ancient pathways that we have been called to walk in (Jeremiah 6:16). As we are continuing to build this spiritual house (Ephesians 2:20-22 AMP, TMSG) we will let their ceilings become our floors in which we build this habitation of God.

We are coming into the time of the greater works generation (John 14:12) and many will arise in this coming season from the secret place of intimacy in Christ to demonstrate great marvels and miracles of the Kingdom among the world. Sadly, some members of the Body of Christ will allow their theological understanding of the Word dictate to them what God is capable of. By doing this they will reject this move of God and even persecute it, forgetting that it is the Holy Spirit that will teach us not their theology (John 16:13-15, 1 Jn. 2:27). God is not looking for Theologians that know Him in Word only, but Oracles that have the Word in them. These are the ones that God will use to carry this coming reformation to this generation.

In this coming hour God is calling forth His reformers and deliverers through deep encounters and visitations, but it is up to them to recognize the purpose of the visitations. For this emerging generation it will not be as much an emphasis on what we see in the heavenly encounters, but what is deposited into us through the encounters that will transform and shake nations. This will lead us beyond where the church has been in the past, causing real transformation to affect whole regions and nations for the Kingdom of God.

These Reformers will answer their visitations with, "Here am I", not simply looking and seeing into Heaven for what is coming, but it will be with the purpose of receiving and releasing to the world what they have been given, authority and power over the earth. In this season, many will have massive encounters in the heavens as God catches them away, with the intention of causing them to live and operate from a higher reality and truth. What we must understand is the encounters we are about to receive are only calling us to explore and live in a deeper realm and reality of God's glory.

God is looking to deposit in this time more than a vision or dream that we can talk about and share with our buddies as we drink a Starbucks on a Saturday afternoon. All of that is fine, but we must come to the realization that there is far more that God wants to get over to us. We are moving into a greater glory with greater understanding of what to do with what we have been given. It is not so much what we see that will change us in the coming days, but what we will embrace and receive as Kingdom truth and reality that will have a lasting impact on us.

It was not until Moses turned aside to look; that God called out to him. He was caught up in an ecstatic experience that caused him to awe and wonder, but he did not stop there. He made a decision to dive deeper into what he was encountering and then God called to him. We are entering past the place of simply encountering and seeing into the Heavens- to living and working with them in a much deeper way.

"And the angel of the LORD appeared unto him in a flame of fire out of the midst of a bush: and he looked, and, behold, the bush burned with fire, and the bush was not consumed. And Moses said, I will now turn aside, and see this great sight, why the bush is not burnt. And when the LORD saw that he turned aside to see, God called unto him out of the midst of the bush, and said, Moses, Moses. And he said, Here am I." (Exodus 3:2-4)

Many in the past have known that change was coming to the Body of Christ and they even declared what they had seen on the mountain of God, but few have turned to go deeper. God is looking for a people that will not only see, but will embrace and work with Him to bring about a reformation. This is what is coming; reformers and delivers to change and shake nations. Both Moses and Isaiah encountered the Angel that burns with fire and answered their call with "Here am I". It was not until they fully took hold of what they were seeing and looked deeper into the encounters that God then released a greater deposit on their lives to Father and equip nations. They moved beyond simply seeing to see, into receiving to release.

We have moved into a decade that will be marked by extreme signs and wonders in the heavens and in the earth and there is soon to be a great revealing of mature sons and daughters on the planet, such as no generation has ever seen before (Rom. 8:19). They will bring a much needed balance to the instability that we have been feeling over the past few years. Those who will come forth in this decade will be known for the power and authority they release over the earth through their words. This is where we are going in the days ahead and the Angel of the Lord is being released to work with those that will turn aside.

These men and women will do mighty exploits for the Kingdom. The nations are going to shake and quake under the signs and wonders that are coming through these mystics and reformers. Many of these wonder workers we have not yet heard of before, but they are coming sooner then we think. They will be marked by great humility and simplicity as they manifest the Kingdom of Heaven. They will be given the Rod of God and will deliver many nations from bondage and cause the desire of the nations to come (Hagai 2:4-9). They will bring a real shaking that will cause the latter house to arise in all its glory and at the same time cause a great stirring and shaking that will cause dividing lines within the Body.

Pay close attention in this coming season to the fault lines. The separation between the old and the new will not come without a price. Fault-finding and accusations will be thrown at those that bring about the reformation, but with persecution only comes a greater release of glory (1 Peter 4:12-14). We must not pass up this coming visitation, no matter the cost. For the sake of America and the world we cannot afford to pass up God's opportunity for us and our generation.

COUNTING THE COST

Controversy is nothing new to the move of God and many that we hale as pioneers of the past such as Finney, Wesley, and Whitefield were highly controversial in their day. Yet because of their boldness and failure to relent on what they believed they restored back to the church the office of the Evangelist and saw true change in their life-time. The same is going to be said of this generation. Those that are coming forth in these days will push the envelope of what some consider acceptable.

Yet while many in public ministry have prophesied the restoration of the Apostolic office, the truth is, that when it arrives much of what we think it should look like and those that are used to restore it will most likely stretch our spiritual wineskins. We better get ready because things are changing faster than we think and what is coming is going to take us by surprise.

We are on the edge of a third great awakening, not just in America, but the world. Yet there are still some so called "famed" preachers sitting and waiting for their next shot at televised revival.

While they sit and wait, a new breed of ministry gifts is arising. They have counted the cost of persecution at the hands of the mainstream and determined to step beyond the status quo no matter the cost. Venturing into uncharted places in the Spirit; risking their reputations to bring the truth, not just to those sitting in the pews of churches, but to the lost and broken of the world.

Much like those early reformers that risked their lives and characters to bring truth to their generation, once again we are going to see many rise up with the same life-force. They will be new visionaries for a new movement. A movement not worried about fame or fortune, but love. A movement not possessed with building mega ministries and huge networks because, let's face it, this generation is not interested in giving to building projects and "church" growth plans. This generation is only interested in funding causes that it believes in. And they will give with more than just money. They will give with their entire lives. Like the revivalists of the past many will count the cost in our generation to spend their lives on Him.

Every great awaking that has come has cost those involved all that they had; money, reputations, friendships, and even mainstream church acceptance. A simple study of past moves of God will easily reveal to us that nearly every major shift and reformation in church history has been rejected by the mainstream church. With this, most leaders felt that what was being preached was simply fanaticism and not the Gospel. This next great awakening will be no different. The truth is that if we are to go deeper into the realm of eternity we can no longer fear controversy and even complete rejection by the mainstream church. It is simply part of the package deal. We must hold eternity more precious in our sight then the approval of men, and the treasures of heaven of greater weight then a seat at the table with the who's who in the charismatic zoo.

COMPANY 81

Recently, while in prayer, the Lord brought me into a vision where there was a knight whose armor was pure light and as I began to look at this knight the Lord spoke these words to me, "The crusaders are coming! Those that I have prophesied about in the past are coming into the hour of anointing and maturity." Suddenly the Lord reminded me of a prophetic word that Bob Jones prophesied in nineteen seventy nine called, "The Sands of Time".

He said, "In January of 1979, the Lord took me in a vision to the sands by the sea and called it the Sands of Time. I saw leaders through the generations sticking their hands down into the sands to bring up boxes, saying, 'Is this the time?' There was nothing in the box. I heard them say, 'Are the promises for now?' Yet it wasn't for their generation. The Lord told me (Bob) to reach down into the sands of time to pull up a box. I said, 'Lord, they are all empty'. He said, 'Open it up'. I was surprised to see draft notices in it. They said, 'Greetings, you have been drafted into the army of God'. He said, 'I will begin to send these letters out to my leaders when it costs twenty cents to mail a letter'. At the time of the vision, it cost only eleven cents to mail a letter so no one ever thought that the price would go up again. But on October 13, 1981, it cost twenty cents to mail a letter and the Lord said, 'Everyone that was conceived, that was in the womb, or nine months prior was literally the army of God. The first would be leaders and the second would be the greatest army that nothing could ever stop and when they reach the age of maturity I am going to begin to release them in power. I will arm them out of my armory in Heaven. There is no gift that I will deny them. They will literally pull down the warehouse of God and they will have no fear of the enemy. They will glorify me beyond anything that has ever been. They will represent me in my holiness and compassion'."

October 13, 2011, will mark thirty years from the date that God mailed the letters to His army; this emerging company, which I refer to as "Company 81", will be those that lead the body of Christ into the land of promise. Much like Joshua did for the children of Israel so too will there be a Joshua company that will arise in the coming days. They will mix both the Spirit of passion for war to take and disciple nations, as well as, intimacy and relationship to stay in the secret place with God. The meaning of Joshua's name in Hebrew is "Yahweh Is Salvation" and the name Joshua is the Hebrew form of the Greek name Jesus. Both Joshua and Jesus were anointed for their position at the age of thirty and as October 13, comes to pass many of the "Company 81" will be turning thirty years old. We have come to a great junction in time, a time of full maturity and anointing for this generation. This will be a Jesus generation that causes a Jesus revolution.

You Smell Like Fish

These new breed of revivalists that are coming are going to smell. They are going to stink like fish! These young evangelists have been laboring in the trenches unrecognized by the mainstream Christian circles. Their smell has been going up to the Father as a sweet savor in His nose, and the persecution they have received from many in the past few years will be rewarded by The Father with great boldness (Acts 4:29-31). They will receive great grace in this season to demonstrate the Gospel with power. The apostle John was an unlearned, ignorant, smelly fisherman that found his salvation on the shore of Galilee. God raised him up to become a pillar in the church and a founding father of Biblical revelation, but he never left his roots of what God had called him to at the beginning of his walk. "I will make you a fisher of men." In this coming apostolic age we will not forget our first calling in Christ, winning souls!

John's strength lay in his pure passion and love for Jesus. His Gospel declared that he was the disciple who Jesus loved. The Bible says that John laid his head on the chest of Jesus. This was an act of love from John to the Son of God. Through this simple act of love an impartation was given of the true heart of the Father. This led him to pen down John 3:16, "For God so loved the world, that he gave his only begotten Son, that whosoever believeth in him should not perish, but have everlasting life." He heard the heartbeat of the Kingdom-LOVE. With all the extreme power that will be released by many in this coming time we are once again going to come to a deep understanding as a corporate body of the love of Christ and the simplicity of the gospel.

We will truly come to understand that it is the foolishness of preaching that draws men to the Kingdom of Heaven, not our great theology or understanding of the scriptures. There are those that are coming that will release what they have been made full of and will impart to this generation the very essence of God- LOVE. God is Love and it is love that draws people to salvation. God is calling His church to LOVE the hell out of this world. This world is crying out for love. Who are we that we should keep this love we've been given hidden within the four walls of the church or worse yet the four chambers of our heart. It is a spirit of pride that keeps us in the boat of complacency. We should be crying out to Jesus on the water, let me come to you. Failure has always been a fear for most Christians, but in God there is no failure. With our eyes on Christ, we will not sink but rise to the occasion and do the impossible through God. We have been called to greater works. These greater works, work by love. Remember, true faith can only work by love.

End the Prohibition it's Time to Drink Deep

There needs to be a whole lot less natural thinking and a lot more supernatural drinking if we want to make an impact on the nations in the coming years. Peter was a wild disciple who made some mistakes, but when he stayed hammered drunk in the anointing he never missed it. There have been a lot of believers that have been walking in condemnation because of their past failures. They are focusing on what sin they committed, when their only failure was they stopped being with Jesus (Acts 4:13). Peter was walking around feeling sorry because he denied the Lord, but when he made it to the upper room everything changed. Here's a word for all those that have been getting beat up by their past. TAKE A DRINK!

If you walk in the Spirit there is no condemnation (Romans 8:1). Peter got to the upper room took a few drinks with his buddies and forgot his past. The next thing they knew he was up on the table blitzed out of his mind winning three thousand people to Christ. We are going to see many that have failed in the past rise back to their positions and do great exploits for Christ. There is a lot of boldness when you drink the new wine of God. Peter was a heavy drinker of the Spirit. The guy drank so much he started seeing stuff (Acts 10). He stepped out on what he saw even when it didn't make sense and opened up a new harvest field for the Kingdom. God is calling us to dream big and think outside the religious box and we are going to see many wild and new ways of winning the lost. The old stale ways of witnessing just won't work in the coming years.

There is so much vision in the wine. Some have lost their vision for the harvest because they stopped drinking and started thinking. They have limited themselves by natural thoughts, when we have been called to have the mind of

Christ. When we drink deep of the Holy Spirit we will see extraordinary miracles in the glory. Even Peter's shadow healed the sick. The guy wasn't even trying. He just stayed in the bliss and God used his body to do miracles. Get ready to see this once again! The best preachers are the heavy drinkers, because when you get out of your mind you are willing to do anything the Holy Spirit says. God has saved the best wine for this hour! This was the first miracle that Jesus did to reveal His glory (John 2:10-11), so let us drink deep of this sweet wine from heaven. " For as we drink of the Spirit in this time we will be changed from glory to glory even transfigured into His very own image in ever increasing splendor and from one degree of glory to another; [for this comes] from the Lord [Who is] the Spirit." (2 Corinthians 3:18 AMP)

Charlie Shamp is an Associate Minister with Global Fire Ministries International and up-and-coming "revelatory revivalist".
www.globalfireministries.com

NO MORE DELAY

by Matt Sorger

The Lord gave me my first prophetic word in 1992, nearly twenty years ago. He said to me, "I am raising up a new breed of leader in the earth." He then proceeded to tell me, "The top of My priority list for you is the opposite of your priority list. The top of My list for you is the refinement of your character, not the fulfillment of your ministry." He continued, "I will cause your roots to go down so deep in Me that when you experience success you will not be moved to the left or the right." "What I will do in the days ahead will be so new and different, you will have to have an ear that hears and knows My voice." This prophetic word from twenty years ago is of great significance to our time today.

I don't think character refinement ever really stops or reaches completion. It's a daily process in all of our lives. But I want to paint a broad picture of what has been taking place behind the scenes over the last twenty years. God has been preparing in secret a "new breed of leaders" that will emerge onto the scene to lead the Body of Christ into a new season and dimension of God's kingdom, power and glory.

NOW IS THE TIME

In July of 2011 the Lord spoke to me, "The time is NOW. The new breed is now emerging." There is a shift taking place in the body of Christ. The cloud is moving and we must move with it. But where is the cloud of God's presence going? God's hand will come upon people mightily in this hour. But what experienced blessing in the past season will not necessarily experience blessing in this next season. The face of the church and the face of ministry is changing. And we must move with the Holy Spirit and discern His heart for this hour if we are to fully come under the blessing of God.

The new breed is now emerging. They are rising up and coming on the scene. Get ready for a divine shift! Character before gifting. Fruit before power. With divine order there will be no limits to Christ being formed in us and shown through us.

CHARACTERISTICS OF A NEW BREED OF LEADER

They will have deep roots in Christ. It takes time for roots to grow down deep into the soil. It does not happen overnight. Through days, months, and years of having the flesh tested, crucified and refined, a deep character is developed. God is going to pour out such a level of His power and glory in these last days, that only vessels that have been through the fire will be able to sustain and carry what God wants to give and release. The deeper the roots, the higher the plant can grow.

They will have a mature and refined character. Now is the season in which we will see mature sons and daughters emerge onto the scene. What has been done in secret will now be placed on the public stage and history will be shifted. The next generation of the body of Christ will be led by mature sons and daughters of God and will enter into their promised land of inheritance.

They will have a refined ear to hear what the Holy Spirit is saying. This new breed of leader will not be program driven. They will be presence led. God is about to break out of the box of our established forms and methods. His presence will move in such a radical way that leadership must have such a yielded and surrendered heart in order to move with God. They will have a refined ear to hear the Holy Spirit and will be led step by step into completely new territory. Sensitivity to God and a surrendered and yielded heart will be vital if we are to move with the cloud of His presence in this hour.

This new breed of leader will be led in a way never gone before. God is about to stir up our comfort zones. He is going to call people out of the boat and onto the water. We must be willing to take risks and move out in faith. Radical faith will mark this new move of God. God will call us out of the familiar and into the flow of His supernatural power and presence. It may be packaged very differently than what we are used to. But if we are led by the Spirit we will be able to discern where God is moving.

This new breed of leader will not be moved by success. There will be such a level of brokenness and humility that marks the heart of this company of leaders, that success will not move them. They will only be moved by God's heart and His will. Their anthem will be, "Not my will, but Yours be done." There will be no competition between leaders or ministries. The servants of God will cheer each other on because their vision will be the vision of the Kingdom. There will be a unity that releases a commanded blessing.

THE DIVINE BLUEPRINT

Matthew 21:2-14 is a divine blueprint for what is emerging in the church. I want to break it up into three sections.

> *1. Saying to them, 'Go into the village that is opposite you, and at once you will find a donkey tied, and a colt with her; untie [them] and bring [them] to Me. If anyone says anything to you, you shall reply, The Lord needs them, and he will let them go without delay.*

> *2. This happened that what was spoken by the prophet might be fulfilled, saying, 'Say to the Daughter of Zion [inhabitants of Jerusalem], Behold, your King is coming to you, lowly and riding on a*

donkey, and on a colt, the foal of a donkey [a beast of burden].'

Then the disciples went and did as Jesus had directed them. They brought the donkey and the colt and laid their coats upon them, and He seated Himself on them [the clothing]. And most of the crowd kept spreading their garments on the road, and others kept cutting branches from the trees and scattering them on the road. And the crowds that went ahead of Him and those that followed Him kept shouting, 'Hosanna (O be propitious, graciously inclined) to the Son of David, [the Messiah]! Blessed (praised, glorified) is He Who comes in the name of the Lord! Hosanna (O be favorably disposed) in the highest [heaven]!'

And when He entered Jerusalem, all the city became agitated and [trembling with excitement] said, 'Who is This?'

And the crowds replied, 'This is the prophet Jesus from Nazareth of Galilee.'

3. And Jesus went into the temple (whole temple enclosure) and drove out all who bought and sold in the [sacred place, and He turned over the [four-footed tables of the money changers and the chairs of those who sold doves. He said to them, 'The Scripture says, My house shall be called a house of prayer; but you have made it a den of robbers.' And the blind and the lame came to Him in the porches and courts of the temple, and He cured them.

Let's look at each of these three sections.

NO MORE DELAY

We are entering a season of divine release and commissioning. The Lord is saying, "No more delay." God has need of His people. Just as Jesus loosed the donkey in Mt. 21 and said that they will let him go without delay. Seasons of delay that have appeared like denial are shifting. It hasn't been denial. It's been preparation. And for some the preparation has been fierce. But there is a loosening coming on a mass scale.

The Lord will release a mass deliverance anointing that will set multitudes free in a moment. God has need of His servants. There is a work for them to do. Many will step into their divine assignments. Even those in their 50's will be released on a new level. Some have said, "God if you were going to use me it should have been when I was younger. I'm older now." But God says, "You are right on time." Those in their fifties and older will experience a new launching into their divine assignments.

Humility & Servanthood will be Mantled with God's Blessing & Favor

The Lord said to me, "I am mantling humility and servanthood." For the last twenty years God has been working with His refining fires in the secret places of men's hearts to purge out self, pride, materialism and other distractions of the flesh. The battles at times have been fierce, but God has used every trial and temptation to refine the heart and produce a quality and character within that has caused roots to go down deep in Christ. This is the new breed of leader that is now emerging.

The blanket was placed on the donkey. And Jesus sat on the blanket. God is mantling humility. The name, power and presence of Jesus will be carried on donkeys, humble vessels of God who know who they are. They will know it's not them, but it's God in them doing the works and receiving the praise.

The House Will Be Clensed

As Jesus went into the temple in Mt 21 He turned over the money changers tables and cleared out of God's house everything that offended Him. God is cleaning house and everything that has entered in that does not accurately represent His heart, He is clearing out. God is declaring that His house will be a house of prayer. There will be a great prayer movement that will sweep through the church. It will be a movement of holiness and prayer.

As God's house is cleansed, we will see a move of power enter in. Right after Jesus cleansed the temple the blind and the lame came to Him and He healed them in the porches and courts of the temple. A greater movement of miracles, signs and wonders will be released through a church that is marked with holiness and prayer. God's house in the days to come will be swept clean, filled with prayer, and will release healing power to the sick like never before.

A CHANGING OF THE GUARD

There is a change of guard coming. As the shaking continues, God will shake the house of Saul as He anoints and raises up the house of David. It's not so much an age thing, as a heart thing. God is looking for shepherd boys that He can anoint to lead in this hour. This Davidic generation will be marked with a heart after God and a heart of honor for the preceding generations.

There will be a greater coming together of the generations. Generations will work together in unity as the hearts of the fathers are turned towards the children and the hearts of the children are turned towards the fathers.

GROANINGS IN NATURE WILL INCREASE

The groanings and birth pangs in nature will continue to increase and accelerate. Some will say that the events occurring in nature are signs of God's judgement against humanity. I believe scripture shows us something different.

Romans 8:19 says that nature is groaning for the

revealing of the manifest sons of God. The concept of a son is different from that of a child. A child or infant is still in diapers. A son is fully mature. As we approach the Day of the Lord and the Second Coming of Christ, nature is awaiting it's final redemption from decay and will get to share in the redemption that the children of God have enjoyed. As we get closer to that Day there is an acceleration happening in the earth. It will feel even as if time is accelerating. Things will move faster and faster. Birth pangs in nature will accelerate and increase. Shiftings in nature will become more frequent and happen in closer proximity.

THE MATURE SONS WILL BE REVEALED

This is a sign in the natural that the Day of the Lord is close at hand. It's also a sign that the full revelation of the mature sons and daughters of God is upon us. Just as when a woman is in labor to give birth, the contractions become more frequent and more intense, so shall it be in the earth. The earth is in labor getting ready for the full birthing of the mature sons of God. The natural is a sign of what is happening in the spirit.

The church will radiate God's glory as never before. The whole earth will be covered with the knowledge of God's glory. The church will corporately be without spot or wrinkle. There will be a depth of maturity in the corporate body of Christ.

Romans 8:14 defines the sons of God as those who are led by the Spirit of God. Maturity in being led by the Spirit will mark the church in the coming days. A sign of this will be the ability to be Spirit led and not soul driven. God is bringing the church to a place of being unoffendable. A depth of supernatural love will mark the church. A love-filled, love-saturated church will transform the world with a radical reformation. Limitless divine grace and power will flow through a humble, love motivated people. Not only will the world see God's power, they will see His face and glory represented in the face of His people.

There will be a great power movement outside the walls of church buildings. But this power will flow through the fruit of the Spirit and through mature sons and daughters who are led by the Spirit. It will be untainted. It will be faith motivated by love.

ASK FOR THE STADIUMS

A global outpouring is approaching. It will sweep over nations and continents. God is saying to ask for the stadiums. He wants to fill whole stadiums with His glory. There is a shift coming of church vision. The vision of the church will not remain introspective, but it will move beyond the four walls of church buildings. The church will be a church without walls. Signs and wonders will be prevalent in the streets.

MIRACLE MINISTRIES WILL BE BIRTHED

Miracle ministries will be birthed through people like Stephen in Acts 6:2-8.

> So the Twelve [apostles] convened the multitude of the disciples and said, 'It is not seemly or desirable or right that we should have to give up or neglect [preaching] the Word of God in order to attend to serving at tables and superintending the distribution of food. Therefore select out from among yourselves, brethren, seven men of good and attested character and repute, full of the [Holy] Spirit and wisdom, whom we may assign to look after this business and duty. But we will continue to devote ourselves steadfastly to prayer and the ministry of the Word.'
>
> And the suggestion pleased the whole assembly, and they selected Stephen, a man full of faith (a strong and welcome belief that Jesus

is the Messiah) and full of and controlled by the Holy Spirit, and Philip, and Prochorus, and Nicanor, and Timon, and Parmenas, and Nicolaus, a proselyte (convert) from Antioch. These they presented to the apostles, who after prayer laid their hands on them. And the message of God kept on spreading, and the number of disciples multiplied greatly in Jerusalem; and [besides] a large number of the priests were obedient to the faith [in Jesus as the Messiah, through Whom is obtained eternal salvation in the kingdom of God]. Now Stephen, full of grace (divine blessing and favor) and power (strength and ability) worked great wonders and signs (miracles) among the people." (AMP)

Stephen was a man of attested character and who had a good reputation. He was willing to serve tables. The Lord released grace, favor and blessing on his humility and character. As he was serving tables the Lord worked mighty wonders and miracles through him. This is another example of how the Lord anoints and mantles humility and servanthood. Those who have a lowly heart, God's hand will be upon and they will be filled with radical faith and power. New miracle ministries are about to be birthed. The baton of the miracle mantle is being passed and God's chosen vessels will emerge from humble obscurity to release the fragrance and presence of Christ to the world.

There is a changing of the guard. What experienced blessing in the past will not necessarily experience blessing now. God is bringing the corporate church into greater maturity. God is shaking pride, materialism and self. The face of ministry is changing. The anointing will be marked by selflessness. The anointing will flow through pure love.

Matt Sorger is a prophetic revivalist who travels throughout America and the nations of the world.

www.mattsorger.com

MENTAL PREPARATION
FOR FUTURE SHOCK

by Munday Martin

What can be said about the year 2012 and beyond? Do many people feel optimistic about this year, and for that matter the ensuing years after it since so many are heralding 2012 and beyond as a year that will earmark a retribution of doomsday, plight, and affliction for all of mankind on earth? Here is another really intriguing question for you if you are a believer in Jesus Christ; should we adhere to a Pagan Mayan calendar that is raising so many eyebrows, and causing so many hearts to fear about this year and thereafter? It would seem the most logical and spiritual answer to that inquisition coming from a people who's faith solely depends on the word of God alone would be no. But go figure right, I mean Jesus did say, "In this world you will have tribulations but be not afraid, I have overcome the world," a little power packed verse we should all look into again if we have given into the subterfuge of all the doomsday predictions and the New York Times best sellers there are out there about 2012 and beyond!

Many books on 2012 showed up in mainstream bookstores in 2011. So many authors disagree about what humankind should expect on s demonic prophesy about the date Dec. 21, 2012, when the Maya's "Long Count" calendar marks the end of a 5,126-year era. What can we say as people of a different Kingdom than this world?

I have some good news for you! We are still going to be here beyond 2020 and we have not even scratched the surface yet in terms of the mass harvest that is coming to earth and the goodness and the knowledge of the Glory of God that is going to fill the earth, and is now. The Lord is going to call a Joel's Army forth in the earth in this time of Global Church reformation and it will be an everyday army of believers falling on their faces before a loving God, knowing their identifies in Christ, and walking daily in their positions in the Heavenly realms with Him. What does that look like? I like to look at it like we are avatars here on earth and the real you and me are in Heaven hanging out with Jesus!

Okay, I won't deny the fact that we are in for some rough times, but in the midst of that will be the most glorious times the church has ever seen! A CHURCH OF LOVE IS COMING FORTH! The one man show is over and a burning company of lovers are arising; a whole new apostolic breed will be brought into the limelight with the heart and intent to promote fathering. Where would I be today if it were not for fathers pouring into my life like Mickey Robinson, James Goll, and Jeff Jansen? Having people like them in my life has gotten me through some of the roughest times in ministry, and also has been a treasure as I have weaned from their wisdom! Instead of climbing up the ladder and kicking it down from behind them, these men have helped pull me and many others up the ladder of ministry and helped give me a voice and a platform to in turn be a father myself to the church.

Now in these times we are going to be required to walk by faith and not by site; a faith that works by love. Having said that, what we decide to "do" as opposed to just "say" will be what counts in the end. If we give mercy in this next era, we will reap it individually and even corporately. You won't need emergency food rations! God has something even better for you than that and will prepare a table before you in the midst of your enemies! If we give judgment, we will reap judgment in the next era. It is in the word of God. God is going to find the ones at this hour who will not complain about anything going on in the economy, the entertainment industry, or whatever the case, but will bless...bless...bless! When they see giants, or dilemmas in a faulty government, or system, they will rise up and manifest change through their knowledge of their son-ship on earth as it is in Heaven.

The greatest shift coming to the body of Christ in 2012 and beyond is the one that takes place in the mind, and that is where the Lord is chiseling. Our hearts and intentions may be prudent, but the mind and heart will have to line up with a tenacious faith that works by love. For God so loved the world...so should we. God's faith in the world is absolutely astounding provided by what door we now have access into that He gave, namely Jesus Christ and Him crucified. So He is asking us to believe in the potential of men and love mankind like he does..."When I come will I find faith on the earth?"

Now on to some things the Lord has been showing me for this coming year and beyond. In the year 2012 and beyond, there will be stock market frenzy as changes in energy and much more will take place. Many people will pull their money out of the stock markets but I personally will not as I am invested for a long-term retirement plan.

But let's seriously get our hopes out of the stock markets and out of social security in America! There is something better than the stock market in the matrix right now, and way better than social security, which I am about to show you. God is raising up something of way more value and it is the value that He has placed inside of you! Believe it or not, until you discover the value that is inside of you, you may never know the fullness of what is available to manifest in your life here on earth. Instead of believers having a "pie in the sky when you die" mentality, we are going to see a major shift in people salivating to see the Kingdom of God invade earth starting with them!

Now in terms of where the gold is going to lie, let's look forward. Here are some interesting investments you will find valuable in the coming years: Companies that alleviate social injustice issues. Let me give you a great example. God will be unveiling the horrible things men are doing though greed and the love of money such as in the coffee industry, the second highest traded commodity in the world just behind oil. Multi Billion dollar coffee companies who pay poor coffee farmers little to nothing for coffee beans in places like Africa and South America, and yet turn around and make huge profits, will be forced to look at Fair Trade more closely. Godly and compassionate coffee companies that care for the farmers will be arising grass roots style and don't just exploit the whole fair trade thing; pretending to be fair trade but are only a small percentage fair trade!

The cries of the poor are coming before the Lord's ears this year! This next ten years are going to be years of REVOLUTION! People who refuse to bow to the status quo of sitting idly by and watching the Mr. D. just ravage the poor and oppressed, our lands, commodities, or educational systems, are going to rise up in holy love and boycott demonic systems in holy revolution. In terms of doing good financially through the coming years, God is going to shift people's mindsets in the body and will be calling many, even in ministry, into the marketplace to alleviate the poor and needy in the world. I myself have started doing this through our web-site at http://www.helpingwithcoffee.com

I encourage you to go there and become involved on our team! We are already seeing God shine on this venture financially for my family and for our ministry as it is a coffee company that is alleviating social injustice issues and helping pay amazing prices to coffee farmers in some of the poorest nations of the world, bettering their quality of life. It also pays its representatives very well as it is a godly company and wonderful longterm residual income career!

I am not going to deny we are in for financial shakings, but I also am going to tell you that God is going to amazingly provide for his people through these times, and especially the ones who see themselves being like Josephs at this hour. There will even be glorious miracles happening in people's homes who serve the Lord Jesus in these times! As food prices go up, families will notably see their food multiplying in their houses. Bread will multiply, eggs, rice, cheese; you name it. Get ready to hear, "Honey, why have we not gone to the grocery store in weeks and our food keeps stretching out and our food budget is not even gone this month?" Yes, God is going to amaze us all in miraculous provisions through these times. God is even going to send angels to help our cars fill up with supernatural gasoline. He will send angels to put new starters in our cars, and be ready to see your dollar of quantity turn into a dollar of quality. Food that is supposed to spoil will last and last! Some might say well that seems silly why would God do a thing like that? Because He is a loving God and he can do whatever He wants to do! Isn't He just awesome? I have personally witnessed God do this first hand when we were giving out food in the poorest ghetto in Caracas, Venezuela! We started out going from door to door and giving out groceries to poor single moms and families. Many Moms would cry saying they were just praying for food that week! Many were getting saved, and wouldn't you know it, the angels thought what we were doing was pretty cool so they came and brought more supernatural bags of groceries. We started out with a small count and we lost count how much we gave away at the end of the day! That night the angels brought more bags of food as they appeared next to the stage at the crusade I was involved with!

Now back to more of what is coming. On a side note, hybrid cars will continue to show very poor ideas in terms of saving money. Gas will continue to go up and down.

We are coming into an age where a new energy is going to be discovered and there will be a major fight over it's implementation, so this will be a very interesting time for the economy, but an amazing time for God's entrepreneurs to come forth and shine and minister to the world of darkness and people under very perplexing cares! One thing I know for sure is do not be afraid! God is building an army of resistance in the body of Christ!

The reason many of you have felt like you are in such a place of warfare and hard times is not necessarily because it is the enemy that is out to get you! In fact, God is allowing many of us to go through hard times so that in this next decade and beyond we will be an immovable army of resistance in the earth! Problems will happen all around us, pestilence, earthquakes, and yet we will shine with brilliance and joy through it all. The church will be taken from the back of the stage right into the front of the world stage because it is harvest time and we will be a people of influence, integrity, power, and love, not beggars, but lenders! One of the biggest things God is going to change this coming year is MINDSETS!

Some of you that have been living from paycheck to paycheck will discover God giving you four to five year retirement plans so you can live off of residual income for the rest of your life and preach the gospel to people of high affluence in the business world, the media world, the political world, and be able to help the poor and fund missions and the gospel going to the nations! Many of you will be called into Media at this hour! Many into full time vocational ministries.

Now will there be an earthquake the rips California off of the face of the map? No! Now let's move on from that. There will be shakings in the Sea in the Pacific, but God is saying do not fear and I am going to protect my people! Be less concerned about the earthquake and be more excited about the shaking coming to rattle the nations in terms of the power of God! Remember when Jesus gave up the ghost after dying on the cross and there was a great earthquake and many people got out of their graves and appeared to many? Man I wish someone would put that part in a Jesus movie! The power of the message of the cross will be revisited in a beautiful way in 2012 and beyond and we are going to see and hear about more "Resurrection from the Dead" miracles than we have ever heard before in history! Don't take those bodies to the morgue! Go and pray for them and raise them up because it is going to happen.

EACH OF THE FOLLOWING YEARS WILL CARRY
A SPECIAL FOCUS:

2012 will be the year of boldness.

2013 will be the year of Conquest.

2014 will be the year of Fire.

2015 will be the year of relationships.

2016 will be the year of mass miracles.

2017 will be the year of cleansing.

2018 will be the year of testing.

2019 will be the year of purity.

2020 will be the greatest year of harvest of humanity the church has ever witnessed on planet earth.

2021 will be the times of the Middle class meltdown in America, but again a great time of harvest in America!

2022 will be a very difficult year and the few years before it, but again, a time to stand on the word and not be afraid!

Don't put too much hope in a United States President to come into office to be the hero of America. That's all I am going to say on that, but put your hope in the Lord Jesus Christ and let God arise in you!

Don't put your trust in princes, but put your hopes in God because the dollar is in for some roller coaster rides over the next 10-12 years. However those that know their God are going to do exploits in His name and will be trusted with great wealth at this hour that will not depend on a falling or rising dollar. Why? God's heart for the poor! Social injustice issues in our lifetime will be trampled down by a new generation that is arising! God is raising up burning contagious lovers who's hearts will burn for the poor and the oppressed. It will be like the generation of the 60s but God will be in their midst this time as huge demonic covenants of selfishness and greed will be broken off of America and Josephs and Esthers will rise up in power and love for humanity and the scepter of Heaven will extend to them in a time of favor.

Mercy will triumph over judgment! I literally see the Spirit of Jezebel being cast down who has had her hand on the world's commodities, and the people of God are going to rise to the occasion called life and shine brilliantly in the market place in her stead! Do not fear the spirit of anti Christ and do not allow panic, depression, or any other kind of mental torment to plague you. Just shrug it off and know that if you are in Jesus Christ you are a new creation and all things have become new in your life. You will be a Joseph company who will spit in the face of temptation, because Jesus Christ will always be before your heart and eyes!

Munday Martin is the founder of Contagious Love International.
www.contagiousloveintl.com
www.helpingwithcoffee.com

GOD'S COSMIC CALENDAR

by Jeff Jansen

It seems like everyone is saying that 2012 will be the end of the world as we know it—change is coming to the planet. Documentaries have been made from the History channel to Discovery about a literal end of the world, speculating that doom will hit the planet in the form of an asteroid, earthquakes, and extensive natural disasters. They claim that this was predicted by the Mayan calendar.

The Mayan civilization was known for their unique ability to accurately predict events according to the solar and lunar calendar. According to Wikipedia, the Mayan calendar is a system of calendars and almanacs used in the Maya civilization of pre-Columbian Mesoamerica, and in some modern Maya communities in highland Guatemala and Oaxaca, Mexico. The essentials of the Maya calendric system are based upon a system, which had been in common use throughout the region, dating back to at least the 5th century BCE.

Maya civilization, known for advanced writing, mathematics and astronomy, flourished for centuries in Meso-America, especially between A.D. 300 and 900. Its Long Count calendar, which was discontinued under Spanish colonization, tracks more than 5,000 years, then resets at year zero.

Part of the 2012 mystique stems from the stars. On the winter solstice in 2012, the sun will be aligned with the center of the Milky Way for the first time in about 26,000 years. The Solstice on December 21, 2012, precisely at 11:11 am Universal time, marks the completion of the 5,125-year Great Cycle of the Ancient Maya Long Count Calendar. Rather than being a linear end-point, this cycle that is closing is naturally followed by the start of a new cycle. What this new cycle has in store for humanity is what many call a mystery that has yet to unfold.

Gods Cosmic Calendar

I believe that the heavens are like a cosmic calendar that foretell all that God has in store for us. Even science has found this to be true and to be accurate right down to the exact second. The early Mayan civilization knew this as well as other civilizations and were able to accurately count and predict times and seasons with astounding accuracies. As this relates to the 2012 date, I believe that they heavens are definitely portraying a point of demarkation coming to the planet. Many see it and are speculating what this all means. The new age community see's it as a shift in upper consciousness that will propel mankind into a God like state of being. I definitely don't believe this, however there is something foreshadowed by the hand of God that is getting the attention of the world.

I believe we are moving into a Super Shift in the body of Christ that will unlock mysteries to the Kingdom of God in ways the church has never seen before. Just as the heavens declared the coming of Jesus Christ the second Adam would come and be the first born among many brothers, so I believe that the Church of Jesus Christ is being prepared to usher in a second coming of the Lord Jesus Christ with incredible miracles, healing's, signs and wonders. I personally believe that we are in a place in human history that great mysteries are being revealed by revelation knowledge and the blinders that have been upon the corporate church will no longer be able to sustain their obstruction as revelation and understand will propel the church forward and she will know the power of Christ in us ... the hope of Glory. The occult sees this paradigm shift coming but the church seems to be blind to it. God always reveals in the heavens first what He is going to reveal on the earth.

The scriptures teach us that the heavens declare the Glory of God (Psalm 19:1). Long before Astronomers and Astrologists were noted for the study of the stars, God had a cosmic time table embedded in the universe that would keep prefect time and foretell the coming of great events. In the Old Testament, Daniel, along with astrologists from his time, knew these things as he accurately portrayed the coming of Messiah in numbers of days. The "wise men" who came seeking Jesus from the far east were astrologers that knew the times and the season of the coming of this heavenly King that was to be born in Bethlehem because of Daniels understanding of the cosmic calendar. They came looking for a "star" and were guided to the Christ by that star in the heavens. That Cosmic revelation ushered in a Super Shift in humanity that resulted in the redemption of humankind by the blood of Jesus Christ, the second Adam. This Super Shift was the beginning of a new cycle and the New Testament of the church. The government of God came to the earth and an era of Power and revelation was ushered into the church. All of this happened by the heavens declaring it. All of this happened within the understanding of Gods Cosmic calendar.

Job 38 talks about the signs of the Zodiac in the heavens:

> Can you bind the chains of [the cluster of stars called] Pleiades, or loose the cords of [the constellation] Orion? 32Can you lead forth the signs of the zodiac in their season? Or can you guide [the stars of] the Bear with her young? 33Do you know the ordinances of the heavens? Can you establish their rule upon the earth?   Job 38:31-33, AMP

1 Chronicles 12:32 says that the sons of Issachar were - Men who had understanding of the times to know what Israel

out to do.

They were men who had a revelation of the times and seasons who knew what God was saying and were able to communicate this to the house of Israel. Today, we also have men of understanding of the times. And more are rising up into the knowledge of who they are in Christ – moving in the authority and the power of the Word and the Spirit.

2012 THE YEAR OF MAN

Bob Jones, a prophet who lives in South Carolina, was shown a vision about the years 2009 to 2012. He saw 2009 was the year of plowing or the year of the Ox. 2010 was the year of the eagle. 2011 is the year of the Lion where great keys of authority have been given the church to unlock the new realms of the Kingdom of God. This releases power over the enemy and power over the natural realm. It's the year of the roaring of the Lion of the Tribe of Judah. But the year 2012 is the year of the face of the Man. Its in this season that all four of these faces will begin to move together ushering in the mobile throne of God. Ezekiel saw this vision in Ezekiel 1 and 2 as saw the Throne of God move with eyes and wings, wheels within wheels that moved where the Spirit of the Lord moved it.

Like Bob Jones, I believe 2012 is the beginning of what many are seeing of a release of Kingdom authority on the earth – through believers - that trumps any other era or age before it.

A NEW BREED OF SUPER HUMAN

The heavens are declaring this Super Shift now, and we are going to witness a coming forth of an anointed people group that move in the upper realms of revelation and power being prepared to bring in and end time a harvest of souls!

They will not do this by conventional means but by will be a new breed of super human, moving with supernatural ability and looking just like their older brother ... Jesus Christ. Jesus paid a price in blood to produce from seed form what will be revealed in these last days as a mature bride that has grown and developed through out the last 2000 years. He is the first born among many brothers or those that look like the original seed. And this company will do the same miracles and greater to reveal the true nature of God in the earth. Jesus said we would do greater works than Him.

I assure you, most solemnly I tell you, if anyone steadfastly believes in Me, he will himself be able to do the things that I do; and he will do even greater things than these, because I go to the Father. John 14:12, AMP

2012 and Beyond:
a Season of Resurrection Power

During a time of prayer and fasting, the Lord said to me, "Jeff, you tell them I'm turning My face toward Wales. One more time I'm going to open up such a revival. One more time, I'm going to touch the U.K." "One more time, the Lord says, "I'm going to release such a spirit of glory and a spirit of sonship in My family. You go tell My brothers. You go tell My family. It's My God and your God. It's My family and your family. I'm getting ready to step into My brothers." I'm going to step into My family. I'm going to step into My family one more time.

I want to read to you a word. Smith Wigglesworth released a word in 1947. I don't know how many of you are actually familiar with this word. This word I believe is a kairos word. I believe it is a word for all of the United Kingdom. This was one year before the latter year rain in 1948. The great white tent revivals were happening at the same time.

"During the next few decades there will be two distinct

moves of the Holy Spirit across the church in Great Britain. The first move will affect every church that is open to receive it. And, it will be characterized by a restoration of the baptism and gifts of the Holy Spirit. The second move of the Holy Spirit will result in people leaving historic churches and planting new churches. In that duration of each of these moves the people who are involved will say, "This is the great revival." But, the Lord says, "No, neither is this the great revival. But, both are steps toward the great revival. When the new church phase is on its wane there will be evidence in the churches of something that has not been seen before – a coming together of those with an emphasis on the Word and those with an emphasis on the Spirit. There will be an emphasis from both of these moves of God after the new church phase. ...And when the word and the spirit come together there will be the biggest move of the Holy Spirit that the nation, and, indeed the world, has ever seen. It will mark the beginning of a revival that will eclipse anything that has been witnessed within these shores – even the Wesleyan and Welsh revivals of former years – the outpouring of God's Spirit will flow over from there and the U.K. to mainland Europe. And, from there it will begin a missionary move that will go to the ends of the earth."

I believe with all my heart that there's something in this land of revival. Listen, it comes from heaven. It has to do with seeds of destiny and those that have made agreements with the Lord by the spirit. Not the institutionalized church, but the true church. The believing church. The overcoming church. Those that have paid the price in intercession. Those that have made covenants with heaven that heaven was able to trust. And, I believe that this land is one of those lands.

In these last days what is going to facilitate this revival is sons that are full of the word, who the spirit of God rests upon, and it's no longer teknon, but it's hulos. This is My hulos, spirit and word. Listen to them. And, the wind listened to them. The earth listened to them. The fig tree listened to them. He gave thanks. He broke bread. He did miracles, because spirit and word come together. He opened up that same vantage point, that same realm, for every one of you to walk in. We're coming into a place of really mature manhood along the lines of Ephesians 4:11-12. It's not about the gifts. It's about the spirit and the word. It's about the hulos. Not, the teknon. Not about the immature. It's about really mature manhood. The gifts were to bring you to that place, to elevate you to that place where spirit and word come together you're a son. Then, the Lord says, "In that day you can ask Me anything you want and in that day I'll do it for you." In these last days spirit and word coming together in mature sons. This is what's going to facilitate.

I'm telling you, God is going to do it from the youngest to the oldest. It's not an age thing. It's not a physical maturity. It doesn't depend on gender. It's a supernatural or a spiritual maturity. It's sons (and daughters) who are taught of the Lord. Jesus was a son that was taught of the Lord. He immediately, when the Spirit of God came on Him, was driven into the wilderness and He was taught of the Lord. Up on the mountain He was taught of the Lord. He was in the presence of God. That's what the desert fathers did. That's what Jesus did. They modeled how to be filled and how to move with unlimited anointing. Abiding in Him and by Him abiding in you, you are a living branch. He lives in you. You live in Him.

You are a son that is taught of the Lord and the elements see it. When you speak, the earth knows it. The animal kingdom sees it. Jesus never announced His Messiahship. Rather, when He was coming across the Sea of Galilee He stepped out of the boat – remember the man from Genasseret? He stepped out of the boat and immediately the demonic realm knew He was there. They ran up to Him and said, "Don't torment us, please. We know who You are! You are the Christ, the Son of the living God. Please don't cast us out into the abyss." But, the demonic realm knew exactly who

He was. The angels came and ministered to Him. They were His best friends. They ministered to Him in the wilderness. They strengthened Him. In the garden they showed up. Every time Jesus stepped out of the boat onto the land every ruling principality and power knew that He was there. And, that's what it's going to be in this nation.

I was in Australia last year, Melbourne. And, the plane was coming down into Melbourne. I was actually going to see Gary and Sarah Morgan. The plane came down on the runway. And, as soon as the wheels touched the ground, the Australian angels came on the plane. And, they began to show me things. They brought me five coins and they had the names of the coins on them. And the angel was standing there telling me about this date and that date and the stewardess is walking through the angel as we're standing there talking. And, I'm mesmerized. I'm always mesmerized when I see the angels. I see both realms, and they're talking to me and giving me names and dates and I see the coins. And, they say, "Jeff, do you understand this?"

And, I say, "No, I don't understand. Tell me more." And, they're telling me more about what's going on.

After they left and I wrote this all down, I said to the Lord, "Why did the angels come to me? Why is it that when I go into a nation and I land that the angels come to me and they start telling me things?"

And, He said, "Well, Jeff, you're a hulos. You're a son. And, they recognize authority and they know you're coming. Because they're looking to communicate the will and intentions and purposes of God in a nation. They come to you because they know you have the power to do something."

And, the Lord just wonderfully moved there in all kind of miracle and healings. There are very few earthquakes that take place in Australia. When I was in Melbourne the Lord told me that the earthquakes were coming. When I went to Adelaide we began to roar. I began to prophesy the earthquake in Melbourne. There would be three massive earthquakes. There would be a governmental shift. As we were roaring, I was prophesying and Perth, which was miles and miles to the west, which is actually the western gate. And, while we were roaring that night Melbourne had a M5 plus earthquake. Two days later Adelaide and within a day a M7.something in Perth. Now, there was very little destruction, but the ground shook. It was like the release of the word of the Lord.

See, creation understands that word. Creation knows that realm. They understand. They respond to the hulos. They respond to the spirit and the word and mature sons. And, they listen and they back it up. Just like Jesus. Jesus spoke to the wind. Jesus spoke to the tree. Jesus spoke to the storm and it will be the same thing with you. What Smith Wigglesworth was saying was there's something key in this prophetic word. All these revivals taking place, the new church movement and emphasis on the gifts of the Holy Spirit and this and that. They said, "This is it." And, the Lord said, "No, this isn't it."

When there's an emphasis on the word and the spirit together. It's not just the word. It's not the word of faith movement. And, it's not just the spirit. It's the word and spirit coming together that brings the mature. Heaven responds and says, "Look, this is My son. This is a mature, hulos. This is a church that has come into a place of maturity. They're not just functioning in the gifting. They're not just functioning in this. But, they're literally functioning as sons, taught of the Lord.

I believe we will see a revival that shakes this nation, the U.K. Even Smith Wigglesworth said. It will start right there. It'll spread. It'll make everything in Great Britain, the Welsh revival, the Wesleyan, all pale in comparison. But, it's going to start there and spread around the world. Now, he saw this. I believe it's a word from God. Do you believe that? I believe that's why I'm here. And I believe you are here for that purpose, too.

Lord, I want to become a throne, a gateway. Jesus, you said to Nathaniel, "Listen, Nathaniel, you're freaking out because I gave you a word of knowledge and I saw you under the fig tree. You ain't seen nothing, yet. He said, "You're going to see the angels ascend and descend. Because, I'm a throne. I'm the door. I'm the Way. I'm a gate. And, the angels constantly are ascending and descending upon Me. And, as I am in the world, so are they. Father, the glory you've given Me. I've given them. As the angels are ascending and descending upon Me, they're going to ascend and descend upon a mature hulos, sons taught of the Lord. Up and down. Up and down. Heaven coming up and down and ebb and flow between the spirit and the word. Up on the mountain of transfiguration. In and out of the spirit realm. The glory of God resting, ascending and descending. Hallelujah.

Jeff Jansen is a prophetic revivalist and founder of Global Fire Ministries and the Kingdom Life Institute in Tennessee.
www.globalfireministries.com

STORM WARNINGS

by James Goll

J esus said –

> "When it is evening, you say, 'It will be fair weather, for the sky is
> red.' "And in the morning, 'There will be a storm today, for the sky
> is red and threatening.' Do you know how to discern the appearance
> of the sky, but cannot discern the signs of the times?" Matthew
> 16:2, 3

We are in process of crossing a historical threshold
in the history of the United States of America. We are in the
midst of going from one room in the Spirit to the next in God's
dealings with the nations. God's plumbline has been dropped
into the midst of the nations to see what character of building
materials we have been using. Evaluation time has come.
As we round the corner to the strategic, pivotal year 2000,
the cracks in our personal, family, church and nation will
show forth to determine if our present foundation needs jack
hammered, torn up and repoured, or if they are solid enough
for God's Last Days House to be built upon.

A time of pressure is upon us. These will be "days
of hardship and days of hope". Times of shock and quaking
change are imminent! For the past five years certain sectors
of the body of Christ have been experiencing "times of
refreshing". But the purpose of these times of refreshing are
about to be revealed - refreshed to be strengthened for what
lies ahead. We have been experiencing a Gentle Awakening;
next it will be the Rude Awakening; and then, if the Lord has
the fullness of His will accomplished, this will be followed by

a Great Awakening.

What time is it anyway? What is the prophetic pulse indicating? Recently, at meetings where I speak or have attended, fire alarms go off in the buildings. One night, when I was on the road in California, the fire alarm went off right outside my hotel room long and loud two times in the middle of the night. Once here in Nashville, TN, right at the close of my message, the fire alarm went off in the rented school building. While in Sunderland, England, at the close of the last nights session, the fire alarm went off! What is God trying to say to us?!

Wake Up calls are being sent through the Body of Christ. Storm Warnings are being issued to the church. The voice of the Lord is beginning to rumble, but soon it will begin to thunder! It's time to build storm cellars of prayer (Psalms 91 and 57) where we will be protected under the shadow of His wings.

A WORD OF WARNING

In April of 1998 the city of Nashville, TN was struck by two tornadoes. It was an alarming and shocking experience with much devastation. The morning after the storms, the voice of the Holy Spirit came to me and said, "If Nashville does not repent, another storm will come." There was an urgency in the message.

Later in the summer the voice of the Holy Spirit came to me again and described three things that Nashville needed cleansing of that all started with the letter "I". He spoke to me that there was mixture in the worship - it is called idolatry. Secondly, He spoke to me concerning the historic place of the independent spirit of pride. Thirdly, I heard a strange phrase that stuck with me, increase for capital gain. (My understanding is that this deals with taking the blessings and prosperity of God just for the sake of selfish pursuits.)

Many of us in Nashville, believe that was simply a "Word of Warning" to our city. A dear friend and co-laborer of mine named David Fitzpatrick, has written an entire prophetic interpretation related to the day the storms hit Nashville called The Voice of God on Deaf Ears that you can look at for detail on this matter. Clearly, the Lord is sending warnings ahead of time! Many other regions, cities and nations are receiving similar wake up calls. But will we respond?

EXPOSING THE ENEMIES SCHEMES

While God is using pressure to test our foundations, the enemy attempts to toss in his two cents worth and create confusion and muddy the waters. In recent weeks, a demonic "spirit of anxiety" has been unleashed against the saints. When this goes undetected and not cleansed, it brings in it's bigger brother named "panic attack". After this is released the door is open to it's big cousin named "terror". There is a confrontation with this "spirit of fear" in it's various forms being waged at this very hour. In these hours, we will need true discernment like never before!

But the Lord has the antidote! Call 911! Yes, I said call 911. Psalms 91:1 promises, "He who dwells in the shelter of the Most High will abide in the shadow of the Almighty." The Lord is our defense - call on His name! Let's agree with Psalms 94:1, 2, "O Lord, God of vengeance; God of vengeance, shine forth! Rise up, O Judge of the earth."

The prophet Nahum said it this way, "The Lord is slow is anger and great in power, and the Lord will by no means leave the guilty unpunished. In whirlwind and storm is His way, and clouds are the dust beneath His feet." (1:3) But his admonishment does not stop there, it continues with a promise in verse seven, "The Lord is good, a stronghold in the day of trouble, and He knows those who take refuge in Him."

DAYS OF HARDSHIP - DAYS OF HOPE

Will we be prepared? Whether it is adverse, strange weather patterns, Year 2000 Computer Bug, global economic recession, or the U. S. materialistic Titanic Ship going under, these times of hardship can become great days of hope. Isaiah said, "For behold, darkness will cover the earth, and deep darkness the peoples; but the Lord will rise upon you, and His glory will appear upon you." (Isaiah 60: 2)

Yes, let's receive the wake up call and get ready! Let's put on our gospel shoes and be ready to tell others of the hope that resides within us. Let us overcome anxiety by a revelation of the Father's great love. Let the Storm Warnings be heard loud and clear. But let us also rejoice - for the Days of Hardship will lead to Days of a Great Awakening!

RESPONDING TO THE TIMES

In the aftermath of the devastation of 9-11 coupled with the series of severe destructive hurricanes, historic Gulf Oil Spill, wars in the Far East, uprisings in northern Africa and Middle East, the devastating Japanese Earthquake all happening in just the past few years – one is prone to ask many questions. In times of uncertainty, the "why" question appears in it's many forms. But perhaps the question to be asking is not just "why" but "how". How are we to respond in such times? Difficult times come – whether it is in our personal lives, those of a family, church, business, city or even nation. But the basic principles remain the same no matter what sphere is confronted or needs to be addressed.

It is my personal conviction that as a nation, at 9-11 and even at the time of Hurricane Katrina – and the great flood of a thousand years in Nashville - we did make a turn "towards" the Lord. How wonderful it was – even though for only a little while – to see churches open for prayer – special rallies held, even stadiums filled in a couple of cities – with prayer and worship. Tears flowed. Compassion was expressed. Humanitarian aid poured in. Life as we knew it – halted for a moment.

But as a nation, we did not actually turn "to" the Lord to be comforted and healed. "Towards" and "to" are entirely different responses. Seems to me a band aid was temporarily put upon our deep wounds and most of us – even in the church world – have gone on with life as usual. What happened to applications of carpe diem – seize the moment?

A RADICAL REMNANT RESPONDS

Of course, this is not the case of a radical remnant of believers who responded whole heartedly to the times. Their lives will never go back to consumer Christianity – they have been changed into producers for the Kingdom. Thank the Lord for all the prayer groups that have taken their place on the wall and all the many mercy ministries that have come to the aid of these many crisis. But to be honest, even this cost counting continuum seems to appear as a tiny peripheral portion of the church compared to the over all stagnant condition of the greater body of Christ.

But what if this is only a "dress rehearsal"? What if there are more severe, devastating storms, attacks and crisis events coming? Have we learned anything? Author Francis Schaeffer taught to ask the right question years ago, "How then should we live?"

STORM WARNINGS HAVE SOUNDED

Times of shaking are upon us. There's no doubt about that one! But could it be that God's plumb line, as in the times of the prophet Amos, are being dropped in the midst of the shakings? The plumb line of God's unchanging Word and of

His character is being dropped in the midst of the church, the nation and the nations. Do we measure up? What chiropractic adjustments must be made in the body of Christ and the nation in order to achieve the fullness of His purposes in this kairos moment?

Storms ... shakings ... turbulent times ... wars and rumors of wars ... conflicts ... terrorism ... are on the rise. What lies ahead? How do we respond? How do we prepare as we see storms coming?

Storms in life and the world seem to take on three forms:

Storms of Consequences of Sins - Our Needed Response: Desperate, true repentance expressed with humility and lack of defensiveness. A realization that we do "reap what we sow" mixed with a foundational belief in the grace and goodness of God. Turn 180 degrees to the Lord and ask for His help to change.

Storms of God's Judgment - Our Needed Response: A desperate cry for mercy is required while seeking the Lord's face for forgiveness with brokenness and tenaciousness. Seek discernment and wisdom. Give Him first place in all things remembering mercy triumphs over judgment.

Storms of Dark Demonic Attack - Our Needed Response: Cleansing from any "common ground issues with the enemy" followed by desperate, authoritative intercession in which we exercise bold faith in the name of Jesus over the powers of darkness. Cultivate thankfulness, keep perspective and praise the Lord at all times.

Each storm in life requires a different biblical response but, in one way, each storm requires the same response - Desperation. Ultimately, when surrendered unto God, every storm can redemptively be used for God's glory, work together for His purposes and even forge character in us.

CALLING FORTH INTERVENTION IN PERILOUS TIMES

There is not a period in history that extreme prayer hasn't been in the forefront of the purposes of God. In fact, in every revival the Lord always sets a people to praying first. Extremist do not hold back but rather cry out in desperation for God to visit them, change them, deliver them, and set free those in captivity. Extreme results are preceded by extreme prayer. History bears this out. Why should this generation be any different?

True authentic revival comes forth when God' people let their inner beings be filled with that which is in God's heart. They open their eyes – they get involved. They let the sights and sounds of pain and the suffering get into their inner most being. Agony and the oppression of a people grips these true believers and they cry out as a women in travail.

Isaiah gave us such an example of persistent petitioning.

Isaiah 41:21-22 - Present your case, the Lord says, bring forward your strong arguments... let them bring forth and declare to us what is going to take place.

Isaiah 42:14 - I have kept silent for a long time, I have kept still and restrained myself, now like a woman in labor I will groan, I will gasp and pant.

Isaiah 62: 1-2 - For Zion's sake I will not keep silent, for Jerusalem's sake I will not remain quiet, till her righteousness shines out like the dawn, her salvation like a blazing torch. The nations will see your righteousness, and all kings your glory; you will be called by a new name that the mouth of the Lord will bestow.

Isaiah 62: 6-7 - I have posted watchmen on your walls, O Jerusalem; they will never be silent day or night. You who call on the Lord, give yourselves no rest, and give him no rest till he establishes Jerusalem and makes her the praise of the earth.

If it was good enough for Isaiah, then it's good enough for me!

Can we yet seize the moment to be enforcers of the Kingdom? Can we stir ourselves to action and actually live the book of James where our works match our faith? Can we have the spirit of Issachar upon us and actually discern the times and the seasons and know how to live?

I say yes! Let's take our intercessory stand on the wall, stir up the grace of compassion and do the works of Jesus. Let's get the whole prophetic movement out of conferences-only mode and thrust forth into prophetic evangelism where the sick are healed, demons are cast out and Good News is proclaimed to the captives. What time is it? It's time to seize the moment!

James Goll is a Seer, prolific author of many books including the classic book The Seer, and founder of Encounters Network.
www.encountersnetwork.com

Seating the King in the American Church

by Theresa Phillips

*And in the days of these kings the God of heaven set up a kingdom,
which shall never be destroyed: and the kingdom shall not be left to
other people, but it shall break in pieces and consume all these kingdoms, and it shall stand forever. (Daniel 2:44)*

We are currently in a season when the world is fixed on
authority and purpose. Governments are changing and
mandates are accelerating at a fast pace. In this state of being,
we are actually seeing Daniel 2:44 emerge as a force that
cannot be reckoned with. This force is set apart by God and
through His divine direction.

This demonstration of the Kingdom is the part in
which the Lord's enemy is seeking to annihilate - and is no
weak link. It is the force that can change the modern world
and defeat the foes of destruction. Even to the coming of the
Lord, salvation can be made sure. Yes, many are called but
few are chosen (Matt 22:14). This means not all are called to
the inner courts - the Courts of Praise; not all have the ear of
the King. One must be summoned for this. That Clarian Call
has gone forth. Many have been called but few have chosen to
hear, due to the lack of knowledge and understanding of the
proper usage of the term "King" – one who is to reign, rule,
govern, and exercise judgment and protect and prosper his

subjects.

Now we, in America, have begun to see the awakening of a slumbering giant! This giant is the church at large looking for position. Yes, it is taking on the position of citizenship of the foreign principality of Heaven. As we see the government shift, we will also see the church shift, although it should be the other way around - the Church has lost perspective BUT is quickly gaining it back.

In the American Church we have something very much in common with the Government of the USA. The function of church government has taken on the same persona as land government; for example, by vote, by placement of leaders, etcetera. This must be noted that this is NOT the way of Heaven. Our citizenship is bought by the blood and by our submission to Jesus. We inherit the right to be seated in the council of our God in Heaven. (Ephesians 2:6) It is through "Christ," the Spiritual Ambassador of the Godhead (meaning Holy Spirit) that we are accompanied to this position, for He dwells in us by that Ambassadorship, and then He Shares that part of Himself with us.

As this awakening is emerging, we are also seeing a vast amount of God's citizens shifting toward a Kingdom mindset, not to be a buzzword but to be a place of enrichment and total fulfillment of life. It is attainable for all; but until knowledge has increased, we will not see the many who are chosen, so we must declare our citizenship to allow others to do the same.

Why? Because it is nearly impossible for the church to continue as we have known it.

So as the shift (looking up for...) takes place, resulting in the opportunity to grow in Spirit and Revelation, change becomes apparent. In the Book of Revelation, we see in Chapter 4, these words: "Come up here." This is vital for the full concept of preaching the kingdom: for the King, for His domain, and His majestic presence is dominant.

As we grow in intrigue and expectancy of the "Coming of the Lord," (Lord here meaning "He is Owner, as in landlord, making him Lord of Lords), we have so often misplaced the realm (Living Palace) of the King - Mansions of Heaven (John 14:2). The Bible calls Heaven "Paradise". It is not Eden. It is a glorious, majestic city made of golden streets and jeweled walls with supernatural beings and living creatures surrounding the Throne.

The Throne is the predominant focus of Heaven. It is the place where decrees and finalities are made. It is His Seat of Righteousness, and we are Joint Heirs in that very realm. (Rom 8:17). We are not only partakers but witnesses to His administrational focus of Heaven to earth, not vise versa.

I say all of this to establish purpose. The purpose is to get you to focus on a concept of unusual ways of thinking for the future in order establish end times actions of greater grace.

As the history of America is studied, we find that our forefathers have established our laws and ways of governing upon the Holy Writ of Scripture. We did not establish a government based on a sole person to lead. We chose a government of a position of rule whereby many people may be chosen to stand in places of local and national government. Our leaders disposed of the tyranny and fears that once plagued their lives. Due to fear, they did not call our governmental leader a king or highness of any sort, but gave the title "Mr. President," a seat of honor made in humility and elected by the people, for the people. It works well for the nation, but it is not sufficient for the church.

In the last 50 years, we have seen an incredible disease related to the Church and State issues. Truthfully, there is a separation of church and state. It is a Monarchy of Rule in the church, but has our present form of government infiltrated to serve the purpose of ministry?

If the two are to reside in coherence, they must be

respected as two entirely different concepts, yet we have seen the latter (meaning a republic point of view known to the world as "democracy") take precedence in the embodiment of the church. As a result, the church has divorced itself for the Reigning King, leading one to believe He is only King of The Jews and will only one day come as a reigning King of Kings. But what about now?

The Latter could not be further from the truth, for if we are seated in heavenly places next to Jesus who sits on the right hand of the Father in His throne room, we cannot deny the Monarchal rule that has been established.

How do we transfer the mindset; how do we establish Daniel 2:44?

As we move into the next decade, we find that we have entered an age of battle for worldwide dominance and positioning of governments. It is imperative that the Body of Christ begin to make its move.

By ministering the Holy things of God, beyond the veil, with a knowledge that is increasing, we have begun a shift to what will ultimately change the message and structure and course of purpose for the church:

1) To awaken man to salvation
2) To train them in the Holy things of God
3) To make disciples
4) To deliver them up to the King of Kings as His Own

Here is the next decade's challenge for the church: to make disciples IN Christ, not disciples of man's ministry.

Understanding leadership, we learn to develop leaders by making one better than oneself and thereby, we have fulfilled: "Make them as One Father as we are One," spoken by Jesus. (John 17). In this unity, we have established that we are all citizens and subjects, proving we have accepted Jesus as King of the Church. No longer figureheads in front of us, but we reign and rule with Him (closely connected).

Once we have determined to transform our mind to the mind of Christ, (the Anointed King = Christ Jesus), we can freely establish Daniel 2:44.

Can the church reclaim its proper inheritance apart from its National Government? I am convinced as we approach the shifting times that we, the citizens of Heaven, must establish a heart toward the King of Kings. The new world order is coming upon us. Throughout the world, nations are coming closer and America is struggling for her place. As one nation Under God, we the people have been given an unusual mandate from our heavenly King for such a time as this.

Seat The King in the American Church; know His Ways before we allow a foreign leader to take HIS Place.

The America, as we have known it, is no longer here; but the Church, as we have NEVER known her, is emerging, as Daniel 2:44 discovered - she will never be destroyed.

And in the days of these kings, shall the God of heaven set up a kingdom, which shall never be destroyed; and the kingdom shall not be left to other people, but it shall break in pieces and consume all these kingdoms, and it shall stand for ever. (KJV)

Glory Be To God Almighty and the King!

Theresa Phillips is a prophetic/apostolic leader and author of
The Monarchy of Heaven. http://www.chicagopropheticvoice.net/

Watch

&

Pray

RELEASING THE HEART OF GOD:
6 PERSPECTIVES ON HOW TO PRAY

From Bill Johnson, Brennan Manning, F.F. Bosworth,
Mahesh Chavda, Heidi Baker & Leanne Payne

by Julia Loren

How you perceive the nature and character of God determines how you pray and reveals your heart. Do you know Jesus as a Lover sent to save the world or do you see Him as one who sits in judgment, condemning the world? Do you know what He is really like? Do you doubt His goodness because you see so much suffering in the world?

Several of my favorite teachers reveal the nature and character of God and offer thoughts on how to intentionally approach prayer during these tumultuous times. Bill Johnson, Pastor of Bethel Church in Redding, California, speaks about Jesus and a God of forgiveness and reconciliation. Brennan Manning, a former Catholic priest, writes about the tenderness of Jesus. Heidi Baker, international missionary, speaks of the love revolution we can start. F.F. Bosworth, author of the classic work *Christ the Healer*, writes about the compassion of Jesus. Mahesh Chavda, an apostolic minister in South Carolina, writes about passing on the power of your testimony. Leanne Payne, pastoral care forerunner and prophet, writes about God's ability to love the world through you. They all offer us ways to pray about the future based on the perception that God is Good.

Prayer should release something into the atmosphere to create change. If we align ourselves first with the heart and will of a good God, we are able to pray the prayers of faith that release the transformational presence and power of God into any situation—personally, locally and even globally. Praying about the things that God shows us is a privilege given to the favored of God. Do we pray to extend judgment or blessing? What is the heart of God? Let's take hold of the heart of God and release the nature of God into the world through intercessory prayers and actions.

God will do through you what He first does in you. Let Him soften your heart and fill you with the knowledge of His compassionate, tender, and loving nature as you read and then release His love, tenderness, and compassion to the world around you.

RELEASE THE FORGIVENESS AND FAVOR OF THE LORD

By Bill Johnson

(Transcribed from May 2011 Leader's Advance, Bethel Church)

"Peace be with you; as the Father has sent Me, I also send you." And when He had said this, He breathed on them and said to them, "Receive the Holy Spirit. "If you forgive the sins of any, their sins have been forgiven them; if you retain the sins of any, they have been retained." John 20: 21

Now all these things are from God, who reconciled us to Himself through Christ and gave us the ministry of reconciliation, namely, that God was in Christ reconciling the world to Himself, not counting their trespasses against them, and He has committed to us the word of reconciliation. 2 Corinthians 5: 18-19

Forgiveness and reconciliation means that we do not hold a sin against someone, that we do not keep a record. What happens in these cities and nations of the world is that the Church has kept a full record of their sins. Statements have been made that God must judge.

I think we need to live with an appreciation for what has changed in the last decades. The righteous are getting sprinkled into every system. The church wants to call down judgment on Hollywood because they're doing stupid things, causing many to stumble, and yet the Lord has anointed prophets to go into the chambers of the King and they are there right now. Why judge now? How about 40 years ago when no one was there? That would have been a great time because there was no one interceding on their behalf. Now He has worked people into the system. Is this when they should be judged?

This is when the entire thing can be changed and shifted because we have people of righteous influence in places of leadership...

There are nations that are under prophetic unction where the leaders are consulting the prophets of the Lord to know what to do in a crisis. So why would the Lord wipe them out right now? It is like planting a crop, waiting until it is almost ready for harvest, and then burning it down. It makes no sense.

We have been given a ministry of reconciliation, which means I look at Las Vegas and I do not accuse them in my heart. I take no pleasure in the tragedy that happens there or in Japan, a materialistic world. How about standing up and saying, "Lord, You've had such favor on us, please extend the favor you've given to us on them."

The Lord waits for this stuff. Sin requires judgment— there is no question. But he put a clause in there, "Hey, if somebody will stand in the gap and contend for them, plead for their case...What I am looking for is for my delegated ones to take responsibility and do what they are supposed to do and cry out for the favor given to them to be extended to this undeserving group. I forgive them. I do not hold their sins against them."

Intercession has taken on an accusational nature and it is not intercession. It is co-laboring with the accuser.

Intercession is to stand before the Lord and say, "You've given me favor and I did not deserve it on my best day, now I am asking you to show the same favor towards this city. Show the same favor towards this person."

Whoever you forgive, I forgive.

When we read of these atrocities, the sex trades, the homosexuality that runs rampant and all this craziness that is all over the world, is our first reaction, "God we need to purge this country of that evil?" Because He gave us the greatest invitation imaginable—whoever you forgive, I forgive.

RELEASE THE TENDERNESS OF GOD

By Brennan Manning

(Excerpted from his book, *The Wisdom of Tenderness*)

As Christians living in the Spirit, we're called to pass on the tenderness of God. The parameters of our compassion extend beyond those who opt for our lifestyle, favor our existence, or make us feel good. Charges of elitism are dropped for the lack of evidence. Peace and reconciliation for all, without exception—even for moral failures—is the radical lifestyle of

Christians living in the wisdom of accepted tenderness. We may be called friends of tax-collectors and sinners—but only because we are (or should be). We understand that we are in the company of some rather honorable people, those sinners; in fact, we are in the company of Jesus Himself. According to the gospel, it's unrestrained tenderness and limitless compassion that stamp our relationship with the Father of Jesus as belonging to the order of the Really Real.

The Lord is in the people with whom we rub shoulders every day, the people whom we think we can read as an open book. Sometimes He's buried there, sometimes He's bound hand and foot there, but He's there. We've been given the gift of faith to detect His presence there, and the Holy Spirit has been poured out into our hearts that we may love Him there. For the meaning of our religion is love. Christianity is all about loving, and we either take it or leave it. It's not about worship and morality, except insofar as these things are expressions of the love that causes them both...

RELEASE GOD'S MERCY AND COMPASSION

By F.F. Bosworth

(Excerpted from his book, *Christ the Healer*)

God is not anything so much as He is love. The most conspicuous statements in the Scriptures about our heavenly Father are the declarations concerning His love, His mercy, and His compassion. There is no note that can be sounded concerning God's character that will so inspire faith as this one. In our revivals I've seen faith rise "mountain high" when the truth of God's present love and compassion began to draw upon the minds and hearts of the people. It is not what God can do, but what we know He yearns to do, that inspires faith.

By showing His compassion everywhere in the healing of the sick, Jesus unveiled the compassionate heart of God to the people, and the multitudes came to Him for help. Oh, how insidiously has Satan worked to hide this glorious fact from the people. He has broadcasted the unscriptural, illogical, and worn-out statement that the age of miracles is past until he has almost succeeded in eclipsing the compassion of God from the eyes of the world. Modern theology magnifies the power of God more than it magnifies His compassion; his power more than it does the great fact that "the exceeding greatness of His power [is] to usward." In no place does the Bible say that "God is power," but it does say that "God is love." It is not faith in God's power that secures His blessings, but faith in His love and in His will.

RELEASE THE GOODNESS OF GOD

By Mahesh Chavda

(Excerpted from his book, *The Hidden Power of the Blood of Jesus*)

As believers, we each have a personal testimony to God's goodness and faithfulness, and to the power of the Passover Lamb to cleanse us from sin. God wants us to pass on our testimony to generation after generation so that the knowledge of Him becomes personal to each of our sons and daughters so that they can take possession of the Passover Lamb for themselves...

Our children need to hear us say, "This is what the Lord did for me." Lost people need to hear us say it. When we give voice to our personal experience with the saving grace of God, we encourage others to believe that His grace is for them as well.

The more we testify of the Lord's goodness to us, the more He will build up our testimony. He will continue to bless us, giving us more to testify about. His hand will be over us in our lives, in our children's lives, in our homes, in our financial lives, in our business lives, and in our creative lives.

RELEASE GOD'S LOVE TO YOU

By Heidi Baker

(Excerpted from an interview published in Julia Loren's book, *Supernatural Anointing*, Destiny Image, January 2012)

Everywhere we go I see people getting completely wrecked. But I feel like God wants to bring this radical, love revolution where people start focusing on loving the one right in front of them and it's more about carrying love everywhere than it's about a meeting.

This movement that I'm praying for is a love revolution where Christians are actually known by their love wherever they are in society, wherever they move, wherever they walk. It's all about breathing, smelling, and walking like Jesus, not so much about a meeting in a certain place. It's like carrying His presence, the glory of His love, out into every single part of society. Where people don't have to ask who you believe in. Because of the way you treat people and care for people they can see who you believe in. Christians are known by their love. And I feel like God is ripping anger out of people, and depression, and fear and causing them to live a life of radical love. That's what I'm seeing. That's what I'm longing for.

It is sovereign when God takes our little hearts and makes them bigger—actually, a gift. When God does that, when He comes crashing in on you in a sovereign way in a meeting, He totally takes away hatred and anger and allows you to forgive people who have hurt you and ridiculed you. Once that happens you change, but then you have to live that life out.

I believe that we need more of those kinds of meetings where the presence is so strong that God literally rips out the hardness of our hearts and puts His heart in us. That's what I'm longing for, more of those meetings. I saw it during a meeting in South Korea not long ago. I saw South Koreans come forward and instead of just writhing and shaking to receive the anointing and wanting the woman or man of power to touch them, they were on their faces sobbing their guts out because God was giving them a taste of His huge heart for them.

RELEASE THE LOVE OF GOD TO THE WORLD

By Leanne Payne

(Excerpted from her book, *Listening Prayer*)

Many years ago I heard of Dr. Bob Pierce, the founder of World Vision, sobbing with his arms outstretched around a large globe of the world. He was praying for the orphaned children of the world. God entrusted him with a special mission in regard to them, and his vision was in line with God's—it was global. He had acquired the Lord's mind on how to pray and how to follow up on those prayers.

This habit of Dr. Pierce's made such a deep impression on me that I now always keep a globe at hand. On first hearing of his custom, I could hardly imagine that God could use me globally. But throwing my arms around a globe, I cried out for God to somehow, in some way, love this needy planet through me. "Lord, love your world through me" is the prayer that has been with me ever since...

Christ died for all who will come to Him; His redemptive plan is global. We are to go into all the world—in our prayers. Then we are all the more effective in prayer for the needs closer at hand.

ABOUT THE AUTHOR

Julia Loren met the Lord while living in Israel and has been in ministry for 21 years. She is a full-time writer, speaker, and prophetic minister who carries a strong anointing to re-awaken hearts to God's love, release the obstacles to healing, and call out destiny.

She is the author of the bestselling Shifting Shadows series including *Shifting Shadows of Supernatural Power* (with contributing authors Bill Johnson, Graham Cooke, and Mahesh Chavda), *Shifting Shadows of Supernatural Experiences* (co-authored by James Goll), and *Supernatural Anointing*, (January 2012). Julia's other, recent books include: *When God Says Yes: His Promise & Provision When You Need it Most* (Chosen Books), *Divine Intervention: True Stories of Heaven Invading Earth* (Tharseo Publishing).

She divides her time between Bethel Church in Redding, California and her writing cabin on Camano Island, WA.

For more information see:
www.divineinterventionbooks.com

juliascribes@yahoo.com

BECOME A "PROPHET" OF HOPE

The world needs hope right now. And you are alive and reading this book for a reason - God wants you to become an agent of hope, a beacon of light, alive with the understanding of who you are in Him. If any of the messages in this book have touched your life, I invite you to become a "prophet" of hope to another and pass the word along.

Here is how you can help:

TAKE HOLD OF THE PRAYER DIRECTIVES AND BEGIN RELEASING GOD'S TENDER, LOVE INTO THE WORLD THROUGH PRAYER AND PERSONAL TRANSFORMATION.

SEND A COPY TO A FRIEND OR FAMILY MEMBER

WRITE A REVIEW OF THIS BOOK ON AMAZON

PURCHASE A CASE OF 44 BOOKS FOR YOUR CHURCH OR MINISTRY (AND RECEIVE 30% OFF + FREE SHIPPING)

For discount info on large orders email:
Tharseo Publishing
juliascribes@yahoo.com

CPSIA information can be obtained at www.ICGtesting.com
Printed in the USA
LVOW062327241011

251786LV00001BB/5/P